Stress Management for Women:

Effective Coping Strategies to Relieve Stress, Worry and Anxiety for Long Term Wellness and Stress-Free Living

Claire Haven

© Copyright 2019 by Claire Haven - All rights reserved.

The contents of this book may not be reproduced, duplicated, or transmitted without direct written permission from the author.

Under no circumstances will any legal responsibility or blame be held against the publisher for any reparation, damages, or monetary loss due to the information herein, either directly or indirectly.

Legal Notice:

This book is copyright protected; it is only for personal use. You cannot amend, distribute, sell, use, quote, or paraphrase any part of the content within this book without the consent of the author.

Disclaimer Notice:

Please note the information contained within this document is for educational and entertainment purposes only. Every attempt has been made to provide accurate, up to date, and completely reliable information. No warranties of any kind are expressed or implied. Readers acknowledge that the author is not engaging in the rendering of legal, financial, medical, or professional advice. The content of this book has been derived from various sources. Please consult a licensed professional before attempting any techniques outlined in this book.

By reading this document, the reader agrees that under no circumstances is the author responsible for any losses, direct or indirect, which are incurred as a result of the use of the information contained within this document, including, but not limited to, —errors, omissions, or inaccuracies.

Table of Contents

Introduction

Chapter 1: Getting Started with Stress Management for Women

Chapter 2: Discovering What Causes Long Term Stress

Chapter 3: Redefining your Life Purpose

Chapter 4: Dealing with Negative Emotions due to Stress

Chapter 5: Caring for your Mind and Body

Chapter 6: Dealing and Relieving Stress in the Workplace

Chapter 7: Dealing and Relieving Stress at Home

Chapter 8: Quick Stress Management Techniques You Can Apply

Chapter 9: Managing Stress in a Relationship

Chapter 10: Finding Time for Yourself

Chapter 11: Taking Opportunities to Recharge

Chapter 12: How to Avoid Mistakes when Dealing with Stress

Chapter 13: Tools and Apps to Use

Chapter 14: More Time Management Strategies

Chapter 15: Simplifying Your Life

BONUS Chapter: Stress Management for Working Moms

Conclusion

References

Introduction:

Balancing work, social life, home life, and personal aspirations and dreams can be challenging for the modern woman. Women are expected to put equal time and effort into home and childcare as they do in work and other roles. The pressure to perform well in all of these areas can cause women extreme stress. In fact, women are more likely to experience chronic stress than men due to poverty, discrimination at work, and traumatic events like sexual violence.

A recent study by the American Psychological Association shows that although men and women report the same average stress levels, women are much more likely to show physical and emotional symptoms. Irritability, fatigue, apathy, anxiety, and headache are some of the most common symptoms among women.

Aside from the above-mentioned physical symptoms, stress can also lead to difficulties in sleeping, weaker immune systems, and worse medical conditions such as depression, heart problems, and obesity. In addition, women can experience problems in their menstrual cycle and/or face challenges in getting pregnant due to stress.

I have personally dealt with extreme and chronic stress. Like most women, I faced gender-biased expectations at school, work, and home. It wasn't enough to be a good student; I was also tasked to complete chores like cooking, washing dishes, and doing laundry. While my brothers were able to focus on their homework, I was helping my mom around the house.

Society enforces these roles on women but not men, giving us more responsibilities. And as if these additional responsibilities weren't enough, society also pressures women to excel in all of these roles—to overachieve.

If you work a full-time job and spend less time with your kids, some will say that you're a bad mother and, therefore, an inadequate woman. It doesn't matter if you're the breadwinner or if you have a six-figure annual income. If you can't make cookies for the school's bake sale, you're still not doing enough.

If you're a working student, you must be self-sufficient and get straight As at the same time. You need to do chores too. You have to learn how to do your own laundry, cook, and clean the house. Even with a stellar average, you're going to have to jump through hoops to land your first job after graduation.

I used to struggle with these different roles and responsibilities too. And it's not because I wasn't good at them or passionate about the things that I do. I knew that. Still, I had feelings of despair and anxiety. I kept asking myself, "Am I good enough?"

But then I realized that all of this stress can be manageable. I can tune out the pressure that society unfairly imposes on women. I can implement a strategy that allows me to balance all of these roles without adding to my current stress level. Slowly, I formulated a set of techniques that I believe can also help any woman out there who is struggling. Not only do these techniques help me manage stress effectively, they can also reduce it.

The strategies that you are about to read have completely changed my life for the better. When I realized how helpful they have been to me, I knew I had to share them with other women too. I started giving advice to my female friends and family members, and they, too, have attested to the effectiveness of these strategies.

For instance, a friend of mine who has three kids and a full-time job used to have random panic attacks. She would feel dizzy, have blurry vision, and hyperventilate at work, forcing her to hide in a bathroom stall until the panic attack subsided. When I found out that she was struggling with stress, I taught her some of my personal techniques. I gave her a list of apps that she could download on her phone, taught her a quick meditation exercise that she can do anywhere, and shared with her some tips on how to take care of her mind and body. She took my advice and told me that she would try all of these techniques to see if they are effective.

A few weeks later, my friend called me to say that she hadn't had a panic attack since the last time we talked. She was in a much better headspace than she was before she applied my strategies. She also encouraged me to write about the techniques that I had taught her. "You can really help other women in coping with stress and anxiety," she said; hence, I have written this book.

Since I wrote this book, I have shared my techniques with other women who are now more happily balancing their professional careers and family life. It's been such a thrill to witness how my techniques have helped so many women to improve not just their stress management skills but also their overall state of mind and well-being.

Stress Management for Women: Strategies to Help Women Manage Their Stress for Success is a book for the modern woman. It contains proven strategies that you can apply in your life to better manage stress and its symptoms.

In this book, you will learn techniques on how to manage stress at work, at home, and in a relationship. I will give you a list of tools and apps that you can use to more effectively manage your time and activities. You will also find common causes of long-term stress and how to address them. Moreover, I have included a holistic approach to taking care of your body and mind. These are just some of the tips that you will find in this book, so keep reading to learn more about how you can manage your stress for success.

For working women. For students. For moms. For women in relationships. For single women. For women on the go. For women who need some alone time. For women who want to do what they love—this book is dedicated to all of you.

Chapter 1: Getting Started with Stress Management for Women

Chapter 1: Getting Started with Stress Management for Women

Picture this: You've spent nine hours in an office hustling to get all of your tasks completed. You've been in tons of meetings, returned hundreds of emails, and finished several reports—all in a day's work. At the end of it all, the only thing you want is to go home and rest. You're planning to spend some quality time with your family before catching up on your favorite reality show with a glass of red wine.

But then a reckless driver cuts you off as you're driving home from work, and whoever's driving that red pickup truck has the audacity to honk angrily at you! As if this isn't bad enough, you get stuck in traffic. The 10-minute drive turns into half an hour! You try to make the most out of it by listening to a podcast, but even the feminist episode you're listening to can't get your spirits up.

"Home," you think, full of hope, as you finally turn the corner to your street. There it is, your sanctuary. You get out of the car, dead beat, but looking forward to seeing your kids and (let's be honest) drinking that glass of red wine.

However, as you step into the house, you're greeted by a jungle of mess. Unwashed dishes in the kitchen, dirty clothes in the laundry room, and school bags sprawled out in the living room! On top of all of this, your kids are fighting about God knows what. Your husband tries to tell you something about his work and how stressful his day has been. And you're thinking to yourself, "Can't he see the mess you're in?"

You head to the pantry to get a pack of M&M's because chocolate has always been your friend. Even though you know that it isn't the best stress-coping option for you, you still rip it open and find comfort in the sweet candy-coated chocolate that melts in your mouth. As you snack with guilt, you think about how all of this will start again tomorrow. Stress is like a vicious cycle—a revolving door that you just can't seem to step out of.

So, you live in your head for a moment and imagine yourself on a vacation in a gorgeous tropical island—sun shining bright, mojito in hand, and the endless sea before you. "I need to get away soon," you think. If only you weren't currently juggling all of these responsibilities, right?

Instead of running away from stress, why not find healthier ways to cope with it?

Stress management is a series of steps and techniques that effectively limits or reduces your current level of stress. It is the central topic of our discussion throughout this book. But before we jump right into the specific strategies that you can apply to cope with stress, let's first examine how stress specifically affects women.

1.1 Women and Stress

Studies have proven that gender plays a role in how stress affects an individual. Women are more likely to experience symptoms, depression, and anxiety from stress than men. Gender roles, gender traits, cognitive appraisal, and biological factors explain why.

Gender Roles

Gender roles pertain to nonphysiological differences between men and women, i.e., they are determined by social constructs and not by biology. For example, the role of caretaker often falls on women. We are expected to take care of the house, our children, and even the elders in our family, even if we are studying or have full-time jobs. These responsibilities bring more stressors into our lives, which negatively impacts our physical and mental health.

Gender Traits

Gender traits refer to behavioral expectations that define masculinity, which mostly describe men, and femininity, which mostly describe women. Like gender roles, these are determined by social constructs. For example, masculinity is associated with leadership, strength, and assertiveness, while femininity is associated with sensitivity, fragility, and indecisiveness. These stereotypes create oversimplified ideas of what masculinity and femininity mean, but they are still taught, both explicitly and implicitly, by society. In several studies, more masculine individuals report better overall physical and mental health. They also consult general practitioners less often.

Cognitive Appraisal

Cognitive appraisal refers to how a person assesses and reacts to different stressors. One can consider a stressor a challenge which, when overcome, can actually produce benefits. On the other side of the coin, a stressor is considered a threat when an individual doesn't have the resources to overcome it. In a study, masculinity is proven to be positively related to challenge appraisal and negatively related to threat appraisal.

This doesn't mean that men are more "up to the challenge" than women. I believe that both gender traits and roles affect cognitive appraisal. Because women have more roles in society, we have fewer resources (like time and energy) to face stressors.

Biological Factors

Of course, biology also determines how men and women react to stress. Female sex hormones can reduce women's physiological response to outside stimuli. As a result, the brain's ability to contain cortisol, which is the stress hormone, is delayed or reduced. This biological phenomenon also explains why women may feel emotional or particularly stressed before their period. Hormonal changes in the woman's body causes premenstrual syndrome (PMS).

As women, we can't change our physiology. We also can't change traditional social constructs overnight. While we're fighting for equality, we should find a way to cope with stress so that we can continue to achieve success in all aspects of our lives.

1.2 Benefits of Stress Management

Stress management can help you get rid of the most common symptoms of stress in women including:

- acne breakouts,
- hair loss,
- weight gain,
- depression,
- insomnia,
- reduced sex drive,
- irregular periods,
- decreased fertility, and
- increased risk of heart disease and stroke.

Stress also causes asthma attacks, panic attacks, and chronic muscle pain and affects memory and learning skills among women. Aside from preventing these common symptoms and effects, stress management will also help you:

- manage time more effectively,
- prioritize urgent and important tasks,
- meet deadlines at work,
- increase overall productivity,
- build healthier relationships with people around you,
- process negative emotions,
- find more time for yourself,
- improve quality and length of sleep, and
- improve overall physical and mental well-being.

If you want to enjoy all of these amazing benefits, read this book until the very end.

1.3 Stress Management Strategies

The first thing you need to do to manage stress is to recognize that it exists. It's here—you can't keep ignoring it, so you need to find effective ways to deal with it. The good news is that you've already taken the first step. By reading this book, you've begun the journey towards managing stress for success. Great job!

The next step is to determine where stress comes from. Take a moment to examine the different aspects of your life—school, work, business, home, relationships, etc. In each area, list the top three sources of stress that you can identify.

Here's an example:

Work

- *Presentation for client meeting*
- *End-of-year sales report*
- *Promotion announcement*

Home

- *Charlie's science project*
- *Look for landscape contractor*
- *Organize closet and laundry room*

Relationships

- *Visit mom at the hospital*
- *Schedule night out with the girls*
- *Ben's birthday party*

This exercise gives you a clear idea of why you feel stressed and what you can do about it. As you can see, most of the stressors above are tasks that are yet to be completed. To better manage stress, you need to first find a better way to manage these activities.

Here's a nifty little trick that I use when I have a long list of things to do. I divide my tasks into four categories based on urgency and importance. There are tasks that are both urgent and important, tasks that are urgent but not important, tasks that are important but not urgent, and tasks that are neither urgent nor important. Then I prioritize them using these categories. Refer to the table below to see what I mean:

Tasks	Important	Not Important
Urgent	Level 1	Level 2
Not Urgent	Level 3	Level 4

I start with Level 1 tasks. In the list above, these include helping Charlie with her science project and finishing the client meeting presentation. Once I'm done with these tasks, I proceed to Level 2 tasks and so on...

In succeeding chapters, we will dive into more specific details on how you can manage stress in different scenarios. But I have found that this prioritization technique effectively and efficiently diminishes my current stress level. I feel more in control about my day-to-day activities because I know exactly where I'm supposed to be and what I'm supposed to be doing at a certain time.

So, the next time you feel overwhelmed or even before

you feel any kind of stress, apply this technique and see how it changes you.

In some cases, there's nothing we can do to control the stressor. Going back to the previous list, I can't dictate how the promotion announcement at work will go. Whether I get promoted or not is out of my jurisdiction. I also can't control my mom's health even though I love her very much. I can be there for her in her time of need, but I can't cure her illness.

In times like this, what I like to do is to recognize that I can't always call the shots. Instead of incessantly thinking about these uncontrollable events and making them seem a lot worse in my head, I focus my time and energy on more productive measures that can actually help me achieve my goals. For example, I can do my best at work to increase my chances of getting promoted and check in on my mom to make sure that she's taking her meds as advised by the doctor.

The Serenity Prayer also helps me to put things in perspective when I am faced with these situations:

>God, grant me the serenity to accept the things

> I cannot change,
>
> Courage to change the things I can,
>
> And wisdom to know the difference.

I suggest that you keep this prayer in mind too, even if you're not a Christian. You can avoid a lot of stress by having the wisdom to know the difference between things that you can and cannot change.

Your Quick-Start Action Step: Download a stress management app or tool of choice where you can write down tasks in their order of urgency and importance. (You will find a list of my favorite stress management apps and tools in Chapter 13.) If you already have them in your phone, use them more consciously. Studies have shown that goals are more likely to get done if you write them down because note taking improves retention. In addition, ticking off items on a checklist is a good motivation to get through the other tasks that you haven't completed.

Chapter 2: Discovering What Causes Long Term Stress

Discovering What Causes Long-Term Stress

There are three types of stress: acute stress, episodic acute stress, and chronic stress.

Acute stress is the stress that you get from current and upcoming deadlines, tasks, and other responsibilities. It is the most common type of stress that people feel, but it usually goes away once the stressor has been solved or dealt with. Common symptoms of acute stress include short-term emotional distress, muscular pain, and bowel problems. Though it has negative physical manifestations, people often appraise acute stress as a challenge and not a threat. In fact, up to a certain degree, it's healthy to have acute stress because it motivates you to get things done. However, if stress persists over time and continues to worsen, it probably isn't acute anymore.

Meanwhile, people suffer from episodic acute stress if they experience acute stress quite frequently. You might be suffering from this type of stress if you are always rushing to meet deadlines or if you feel like your to-do list isn't getting shorter. However, unlike acute stress, episodic acute stress is more likely caused by your personality and not by external factors. People with competitive and self-critical personalities who are in a constant sense of urgency (which psychologists may refer to as Type A behavior pattern) usually suffer from it.

The last type of stress is chronic or long-term stress. In this chapter, we will focus on its causes, effects, and how to manage it effectively.

2.1 Long-Term Stress

Have you ever felt like you can't find a way to get out of your predicament? Have you ever felt stuck in a situation that you just don't want to be in anymore? Have you ever felt like you don't have the resources to solve your problems?

When a person feels hopeless about her situation, she is most likely dealing with chronic stress. This is the type of stress that stays long term even when the stressor has passed. In some cases, chronic stress can start to feel familiar and comfortable, which is when a person loses the motivation to find a solution to her problems. She just accepts stress and the symptoms that she is currently living with instead of looking for a way to change her reality.

The most common signs and symptoms of stress include:

- weaker immune system,
- fluctuating appetite,
- sudden weight loss or weight gain,
- fatigue,
- migraines,
- insomnia,
- extreme irritability,
- inability to concentrate,
- helplessness, and
- lower self-esteem.

A person who has chronic stress can also experience an increase in addictive behaviors such as binge eating, teeth grinding, impulse buying, drinking alcohol, smoking, and/or using drugs and other related substances. As a result, she faces an increased risk of developing the following physical and mental health problems:

- high blood pressure
- heart disease
- diabetes
- obesity
- autoimmune diseases
- clinical depression
- general anxiety disorder
- schizophrenia

Chronic stress can also lead to burnout. A person may lose interest in activities that she used to find entertaining or fulfilling. She may begin to distance herself from friends and family, which can make her physical and mental state even worse.

2.2 Causes of Long-Term Stress

Where does long-term stress come from? Chronic stress can arise from a lot of different sources, including traumatic events, financial problems, and relationship problems.

Traumatic Events

Traumatic events such as bullying, sexual violence, domestic abuse, military combat, horrific accidents, terrorist attacks, and natural disasters can lead to post-traumatic stress disorder (PTSD). There are three types of PTSD—mild, moderate, and severe—although these categories don't speak to how terrible the traumatic event was. They simply describe the impact of the trauma to someone's life.

Common symptoms of PTSD include vivid flashbacks of the traumatic event, feelings of being constantly on the edge, unhealthy distractions like staying busy or feeling detached, and unhealthy beliefs like being unable to trust anyone or feeling unsafe everywhere.

Financial Problems

Financial problems like poverty, sudden loss of

income, loss of property, business bankruptcy, and accumulating too much debt can lead to chronic stress. Around the world, about 736 million people live in extreme poverty, with single mothers and older women at higher risks. Household debt has reached $4.6 trillion in China, $1.4 trillion in South Korea, $2 trillion in the United Kingdom, $15.4 trillion in the United States, and $1.6 trillion in Canada.

Poverty-related stress has been proven to contribute to worsening symptoms for delinquency, attention problems, somatic complaints, and anxiety and/or depression.

Relationship Problems

Relationship stress, especially in marriages, can turn into chronic stress if both parties refuse to deal with it as soon as they can. At the same time, stress can be the cause of worsening relationship problems. Either way, stress-related relationship problems lead to lack of support, less intimacy, less satisfaction in the relationship, and isolation.

Aside from traumatic events, financial problems, and relationship problems, chronic stress can also be caused by work, school, and discrimination based on gender, race, and other grounds. Undiagnosed mental health disorders may also lead to this type of stress.

2.3 Managing Long-Term Stress

If you suffer from chronic stress, there are several ways to manage it in order to limit its effects in your life. Here is a general guide to managing long-term stress:

1. Assess if your stress is chronic or not. Is it short term, i.e., it comes and goes with a given stressor? Or is it long term, i.e., it stays even after the stressor is gone? If you answered yes to the latter question and have several signs and symptoms as listed beforehand, then you may be suffering from chronic stress.

2. Determine what the stressor is. Did you experience a traumatic event? Are you having financial or relationship problems? Could there be another source of stress in your life?

3. Confide in someone. One of the best things that you can do for yourself if you have chronic

stress is to talk about it so that you can process it in a healthier way and not make it worse in your head. There are several ways that you can open up about chronic stress:

    a. If you have the means, consult a therapist and make therapy a regular habit.

    b. Seek the help of a social worker if you have financial problems and can't afford therapy.

    c. Join a support group. Surrounding yourself with people who are going through the same challenges will make you realize that you're not alone. Peer support will also help you find your voice and make you more accountable.

4. Find a way to deal with chronic stress as it relates to the source. To help you with this step, I have listed some practical suggestions on how you can manage chronic stress given the stressors that we identified earlier.

Traumatic Events

Post-traumatic stress disorder is a recognized mental health problem. Here are some ways to help yourself if you live with PTSD:

- Identify your triggers. What things, places, or events cause vivid flashbacks of the traumatic event?

- Develop a coping mechanism for flashbacks. For example, you can keep a diary to track your physical and mental responses to triggers around you. You can practice mindful breathing to prevent panic attacks. You can carry an object that has sentimental value, like a piece of jewelry, which you can touch or look at until the flashback subsides.

- Spend more time outside so you can prevent isolating yourself from the rest of the world. Hiking, jogging, and biking in nature are some activities that will not only help you mentally but also physically.

- Give yourself time to heal. It's normal to feel stress after a traumatic event so don't push yourself to feel better instantly. You also don't have to tell people about what happened if you're not ready. At your own pace, you will find the strength to finally talk about your trauma.

Financial Problems

Financial problems come in a lot of different forms, but we'll focus on personal financial management in this section. There are three simple ways that you can change your financial habits:

- Keep a record of your spending. By tracking how you spend your money, you'll have an overview of your biggest expenses so that you can make adjustments in your budget if needed.

- Avoid temptations. For each purchasing decision, ask yourself: "Do I need this?" If you can live without the item that you want to buy, you probably shouldn't spend your money on it, especially when you're already in the midst of a personal financial slump.

- Apply the prioritization technique that I taught you in Chapter 1 to your personal budget. Allot resources to your urgent and important needs first, to your urgent but unimportant expenses second, to your important but not urgent needs third, and to your unimportant and not urgent expenses last. This technique ensures that you have enough resources for your basic needs (like rent, food, utilities, and other bills) before you spend money on unnecessary items.

- Identify your financial stressors. What causes you the most stress in your budget? How can you slowly eliminate these stressors? For instance, if you have unpaid credit card bills, try not to use your credit card until all of your debt has been paid off.

Relationship Problems

We will talk about stress in relationships in more detail later on. You'll find healthy ways to manage this type of stress in Chapter 9.

Your Quick-Start Action Step: Take a moment to assess your stress and determine whether it's chronic or not. Use the general guideline that we talked about in the previous section to start managing long-term stress.

Chapter 3: Redefining your Life Purpose

Chapter 3: Redefining Your Life Purpose

Imagine driving down a winding rural road in the middle of the night. You're desperately trying to find your way back to the city, but you don't have reception so you can't use your phone for navigation. Pine trees stand tall on either side of your car like cage bars. With your high-beam headlights on, you can still only see several feet ahead of you. You wonder how long this journey will take because you have no idea which direction is the right one. Every fork in the road is a gamble. You try to use your intuition as a guide, but you're uncertain of how reliable it can be given how dark everything is. Anxiety starts to build inside you when you realize that you might be lost.

Stress, especially chronic stress, can stem from a lack of direction. Like driving down a dark road without a map, you're blindly going through life without a purpose.

In this chapter, we will talk about the importance of finding your life purpose. How does it affect your wellness? And how do you find a new direction when you feel lost or uncertain about the path you're currently taking?

3.1 Wellness and Purpose

There's a reason why science and religion are keen in explaining where existence came from—the beginning of all creation gives us an idea of why we're all here. In other words, it tells us our purpose.

In science, we study the Big Bang Theory and the Darwin Theory of Evolution. The former explains that the universe expanded from a small, hot, and dense state. This process created our planet, our sun, our galaxy, and all other celestial bodies in the universe. Meanwhile, the latter explains that we all evolved from a single-cell organism that went through different stages of modification for thousands of years. Through natural selection, your ancestors survived famines, pandemics, and wars to give birth to your grandparents who gave birth to your parents who gave birth to you.

In religion, particularly in Judaism and Christianity, we learn about a Supreme God who created everything in the universe in under a week. This includes Adam and Eve and every living species on the planet. The Bible teaches us that we're special because God created man in His image, and so it isn't an accident that you're here.

You can search for meaning in these terms, but finding your purpose can also be a personal journey. The human condition is broad and unique at the same time; we all share common experiences, but our individual stories are exceptionally our own.

So, what is *your* life purpose?

Some may say that their purpose in life is to be happy. You can look for a job that makes you happy, marry a partner who makes you happy, build a home that makes you happy, and all will be well in life.

But what happens in between these milestones?

Even if you land your dream job, stressors are still present. Deadlines, meetings, and workplace politics can lead to a ton of stress.

Even if you find your dream partner, no relationship is perfect. Misunderstandings, disagreements, and uncertainty are common in any long-term relationship.

Even if you buy your dream house, problems can still arise. Mortgage payments, repairs, and home maintenance are all a huge financial responsibility.

So instead of pursuing a feeling, I suggest that you pursue meaning. Like Kaplin and Anzaldi (2015) said, "Meaningfulness is more enduring than happiness and can sustain people through periods of stress and suffering." I couldn't agree more with this sentiment. Your purpose must be driven by meaning if you want to live a well-rounded life.

In terms of how purpose affects wellness, Johnston (2012) discovered in a study that purpose allows individuals to find "value and satisfaction in their lives, both for themselves and a greater being." In addition, purpose improves someone's thoughts, feelings and behaviors, provides drive and motivation to achieve goals, and prevents risky behaviors such as drinking alcohol and taking drugs. It can also help someone in recognizing the "holistic nature of health and well-being."

If you have a clear purpose, you will have a better understanding of the direction that you want to take in life. And if you know which direction you're heading to, it will be easier to think of actionable steps that can take you closer towards your goals.

In other words, you can make a wellness plan that serves your ultimate purpose. Physically, mentally, socially, and in all other aspects of your life, you will have a direction. You don't need to drive aimlessly anymore.

3.2 Benefits of a Wellness Plan

Why do you need a wellness plan in order to fulfill your purpose? Well, let's go back to our example at the beginning of the chapter.

You're driving because you have a destination. You won't reach your destination without a car. Your car won't get to the destination if it doesn't have enough gas. You won't be able to see your way if the car doesn't have working headlights.

Moreover, you would have known before the trip that the reception might be bad given the route that you're going to take. You would have prepared another navigational system to help you find your way. Why are you driving in the middle of the night anyway? Had you planned for the trip, you would have accounted for all of these challenges before you left your starting point.

Do you see what I'm trying to say? In fulfilling your purpose, a wellness plan will help you:

- outline the journey from your starting point to your goals,
- have an overview of which direction your life is taking,
- prepare everything you need before you start the journey,
- have more control on how you want to proceed at every fork in the road, and
- make adjustments if ever there are unforeseen circumstances that derail your original plan.

3.3 Finding Your New Direction

The biggest mistake that people make when creating a

wellness plan is being too broad about the actions that they're planning to take. When your goals are too broad, too big, or too unrealistic, you tend to get off track. You stop following your wellness plan. I mean, have you ever created a list of New Year's resolutions? How did that pan out?

So, try to be as specific as possible. Set the bar realistically so that you don't have to keep leaping in order to make progress. As you move forward, you can adjust your expectations based on your current performance. The most important thing is that you're moving forward. You're taking steps towards your ultimate goals. No matter how slow the pace is, it doesn't matter. You just have to get the ball rolling and the momentum will keep you going.

To create a wellness plan, here are a few steps:

1. Divide your wellness plan into sections. You can use different aspects of your life as categories, i.e., physical health, mental health, habit formation, financial growth, relationships, etc.

2. Use the SMART method to identify your main goals for each aspect. SMART stands for specific, measurable, attainable, relevant, and time based. I will give you an example for each later on.

3. Once you've identified your goals, list a few actionable steps that you can take in order to achieve them.

4. Set a deadline for your actions if applicable. You can choose a specific date for some goals and have a ballpark for others.

5. Identify challenges that may come along the way and prepare a contingency plan.

So, let's say that I'm writing the mental health portion of my wellness plan. For the sake of our discussion, let's say that I have chronic stress rooted in a past trauma. My purpose is to live and function as a healthy human being who is free from the chains of the past. Therefore, my goals will be:

- Specific - to consult a psychiatrist
- Measurable - to keep track of my triggers

- Attainable - to join a support group
- Relevant - to find a healthy coping mechanism
- Time based, to take my meds regularly

The actionable steps that I'm planning to take are:

- Specific - to consult a psychiatrist
    - Find a psychiatrist nearby. Have a list prepared by Friday.
    - Schedule an appointment for next week.
    - Prepare questions about therapy, medications, and other coping mechanisms. Have questions ready before appointment.
- Measurable - to keep track of my triggers
    - Keep a diary of things, places, and people that trigger me.
    - Answer these: Why do they trigger me? What happens when I'm triggered?
- Attainable - to join a support group

- Find a support group nearby. Make a Google search ASAP.
- Attend the next meeting.
- Make connections with other members when I've chosen a support group to join.

- Relevant - to find a healthy coping mechanism
    - Perform mindful breathing when a panic attack happens.
    - Work on my physical fitness starting Monday (refer to Physical Health section of my wellness plan).
    - Start a hobby, like painting, so I don't obsess over the traumatic event.
- Time based, to take my meds regularly
    - Buy meds before I go home.
    - Set an alarm for when I need to take them.

The challenges I might encounter include:

- The therapy might be too expensive for me.
- I may not have time to work on my physical fitness and to start a hobby at the same time.

My contingency plan is to:

- Look for a social worker or a less expensive psychiatrist.
- Adjust my schedule to make time for workouts.
- Paint only when the obsession gets really bad. Otherwise, take a walk, go out with a friend, or watch a movie to take my mind off of the traumatic event.

This is just an example of what a wellness plan looks like. As you can see, all of these goals and steps point towards a single purpose, which is what I set out earlier.

Your Quick-Start Action Step: Create a wellness plan that you can actually stick to. It doesn't need to be perfect, but it must help you achieve your ultimate purpose.

Chapter 4: Dealing with Negative Emotions due to Stress

Chapter 4: Dealing with Negative Emotions due to Stress

Stress evokes negativity that can affect our mental health and overall well-being. It's normal for us to feel negative emotions when stress becomes a threat. But it's common for a lot of people to ignore these negative emotions because there are usually other and more important things that we need to focus on. Ignoring them is how we turn on the fight-or-flight switch in our brains; we can either succumb to the negativity or push through it so we can finish all of our tasks and meet our deadlines.

However, it isn't healthy or sustainable to keep ignoring negative emotions that come from stress. All of these pent-up emotions will eventually find their way out of your chest, and it will be a worse disaster when they do. It is imperative to not only recognize that these negative emotions exist but to also confront them. We need to process them so that they don't snowball into a much bigger problem that will be too much for us to handle.

In this chapter, we will talk about stress-related negativity and how you can change your mindset even in the midst of stress.

4.1 Stress-Related Negativity

Our stress response begins in the brain where the amygdala, after sensing a stressor, sends a signal to the hypothalamus. The hypothalamus then sends a message to the rest of the body to let us know if we need to fight or flee. After receiving the message, our body responds to the stressor. Faster breathing and heartbeat, higher blood pressure, and dilated eyes are some of the common physical responses to stress. We may also get a burst of energy or adrenaline rush if the hypothalamus triggers a flight response. This allows us to get out of immediate danger.

But stress can also take a different kind of toll on our emotions. A study has shown that negative emotional responses to daily stressors result in emotional distress and psychological disorders in the long run. Mental health problems don't just arise from major life events; stress and its corresponding emotional cost can be detrimental to our mental health as well.

Anger, fear, desperation, inferiority, misery, uncertainty, and frustration are just a few examples of emotional responses to stress. We also talked in preceding chapters of this book about how stress can lead to irritability, depression, and anxiety. These negative emotional responses, when not given proper attention, can get worse over time.

4.2 Importance of Recognizing Stress-Related Negativity

Together, stress and negativity are like a self-fueling machine. Stress leads to negativity. Negativity leads to more stress. If you don't change your mindset, you'll just keep running in circles.

It is important to recognize and process stress-related negativity because it allows you to break the cycle. Aside from that, a positive mindset can also lead to:

- a longer life span,
- a stronger immune system,
- a lower depression rate,
- reduced risks of cardiovascular diseases, and

- overall healthier physical and psychological states.

4.3 Changing Your Mindset

There are four common ways that we get stuck in our head, allowing negative emotions to fester and become much worse than they actually are: regret, old ideas, righteousness, and blaming thoughts for behaviors.

- Regret is good up to a certain degree because it allows us to learn from our past mistakes. However, when we let too much regret damage our self-image and cause anxiety over future decisions, we create unnecessary stress that leads to other negative emotions and vice versa.

- Believing old ideas that don't fit our current situation, like doubting ourselves at work when we've been promoted or praised for our performance, is a difficult habit to break.

- Righteousness, or the desire to be right in every argument, can cause stress in all types of relationships.

- Blaming thoughts for behaviors hinders personal growth. For example, you can say that you're an anxious person. This thought stops you from making friends, participating in group activities, and attending social events.

With all these challenges, is it really possible to live with a positive mindset, even if we're experiencing stress every day? The answer is yes. There are several changes that you can make so that you can have a more positive general outlook in life. Here are some of my suggestions:

- Understand your emotions—not just how you feel but also why you feel a certain way. Where is your anxiety coming from? Why are you compelled to stick to old ideas? What past mistake is causing all of this regret?

- Find an outlet like meditation, exercise, or creative endeavors to keep negative emotions away. Better yet, use these outlets to process emotions instead of pushing them away. Set healing as your intention during meditation, express your unspoken feelings through art, etc.

- Be more compassionate towards yourself. You may have made mistakes in the past, but you can't let regret control your life. Think: What lessons did you learn from the mistake? Did the mistake ultimately lead to personal growth?

- When in a disagreement with someone, try to focus on your emotions instead of being right. Use "I feel" sentences instead of "I know" declarations and/or accusations. To illustrate, instead of saying, "I knew your method was wrong. You should have listened to me," try saying, "I felt unheard. My suggestions were ignored."

- If you want to face unhealthy thoughts head on, you can do things that negate them. For example, you can ask a few coworkers to join you for Friday night drinks if you think that your anxiety is hindering your socialization skills.

- Change any pattern of behavior that leads to negative emotions. For instance, you can avoid unnecessary stress if you stop procrastinating. Manage your time more wisely so you can get through all of your tasks before their deadlines. (You can find time management tips in [Chapter 14](#).)

These are just some of the ways that you can deal with stress-related negativity. Use my suggestions as a guide, but it is still up to you to find coping mechanisms that work for your situation.

Your Quick-Start Action Step: Figure out why you are stuck with negative emotions, then apply the appropriate solution from the suggestions that I presented earlier. You may also come up with your own coping mechanisms. You can use the SMART method from the previous chapter to do so.

Chapter 5: Caring for your Mind and Body

Chapter 5: Caring for Your Mind and Body

So far, we've discussed how stress, especially chronic stress, can affect your overall well-being. We also established the significance of a life purpose in preventing chronic stress and the importance of dealing with negative emotions brought about by stress. The first four chapters of this book laid the foundation for our ongoing discussion.

But before we dive into specific stress scenarios (i.e., workplace, home, and relationships), I want to share with you a holistic approach to caring for your mind and body. The techniques that you will learn from this chapter will equip you in every stressful situation so that you can more confidently reach for success.

5.1 Mind and Body

How do you define what health is? Is being healthy simply being free of sickness or diseases? Personally, I believe that health is a positive overall state of physical, mental, and social wellness. Therefore, the presence of stress, especially when it starts to affect your physical and mental state in the long run, is not healthy.

High cortisol levels can impede cognitive function and have dire effects on the brain's physiology. It can disrupt synapse regulation, kill brain cells, and reduce the size of the prefrontal cortex, which is responsible for memory and learning. Stress also affects the body. Chronic muscle pain, cardiovascular diseases, and reproductive problems result from excessive stress.

To complete tasks and excel in all of our roles, we rely on both mind and body. When stress slows down either or both of them, it's a lot harder to function as a productive human being.

Stress can also get in the way of balance. Our minds and bodies may go against each other when we are under a lot of pressure. Even though we have the physical strength to work, mental exhaustion prevents us from fulfilling what is required of us. At the same time, even though our mental faculties are at full power, physical exhaustion forces us to stay in bed and rest.

To illustrate my point further, imagine buying a rundown house. The yard is a jungle, the interior design is outdated, and there are a couple of problems, like water damage, old carpets, and peeling paint, that need to be fixed. But you still made an offer because the house has nice bones. There's hardwood floor underneath the dusty beige carpet, the rooms are the right size, and the floor plan is exactly what you're looking for.

After signing the paperwork and getting the keys to the house, you're ready for renovation. You have a long list of things that you want to change, like repainting the whole house, retiling the bathroom, and putting in new kitchen cabinets and appliances.

But before you can even start the demo, the contractor walks up to you and says, "What's your plan for the attic?"

"The attic?" you say, totally surprised.

"Yes, the attic. It has water damage, too. If we don't fix it, the whole ceiling might cave."

You didn't know that the house has an attic, much less that it's in poor condition. The contractor wonders why you didn't know about it before you bought the house. But he reminds you that there's nothing you can do about it now. There's an attic, it has water damage, and you need to do something about it.

So, he asks, "What's the plan?"

Do you proceed with the renovation and ignore the attic? Or do you fix it before you continue with the rest of the house?

If you choose the first scenario, there is a possibility that the wood in the attic will rot, causing the ceiling to cave and leading to more damage and possible danger to the residents of the house. The truth is you'll always be stressed about living in the house and worrying about whether the ceiling will fall on you or not if you leave the attic unfixed. It won't matter how pretty, sparkly, and brand new the rest of the house is.

Now imagine buying a secondhand car. You decided to purchase a 2006 Mini Cooper from a friend because the engine is in great shape and the mileage is low for its age. Plus, the price is lower than your budget. Even if your friend informs you that the tires need to be changed because the treads are a little worn off, you still get the car because you think that it's in pretty good condition, especially for its price.

So, you take the car to a mechanic to get the tires changed. However, you find out that the airbags need to be replaced and that there are other repairs that need to be done in the interior as well. After assessing the car, the mechanic gives you a quote for all the repairs, which is much higher than you expected.

You have to make a decision: Do you get the tires and interior repaired? Or do you rely on the engine alone and trust that it's enough to take you where you want to go?

Of course, you already know the answer—you need to make the repairs. Even if the engine runs smoothly, the whole car won't function properly if you neglect the problems that currently exist in the body.

In the first example, the mind is the attic. Your body can look as polished and presentable as you want it to seem. But if your mental state is not in a good place, you'll never feel secure.

In the second example, the tires and the interior refer to the body. The engine, which is the mind, can be in great condition but the car, which is you, will not run properly if the body is not in shape.

The mind and the body always work in tandem. You can't achieve success if you ignore one of them. Therefore, when finding ways to take care of yourself, you need to consider both your mind and body. Instead of working on single solutions, work on a holistic approach.

5.2 Benefits of a Holistic Approach to Well-Being

A holistic approach to well-being, also called holistic health, combines different methods of caring for the mind and body in order to achieve overall wellness. Aside from its ultimate goal, holistic health has two other key benefits:

- A holistic approach to well-being addresses stress and solves it from the root cause. You are not just looking for quick solutions to address the problem. It will push you to change your habits, diet, and activities so that you can work towards a long-term goal.

- A holistic approach to well-being promotes education. You are encouraged to learn about the problem, its causes, and its effects so you can come up with appropriate solutions that work well together.

In addition, holistic health takes into consideration both your mental and physical wellness. As a result, you feel good about yourself and are able to meet the demands of life. It also helps you improve your quality of life and can even lengthen your lifespan.

5.3 Tips for Mind and Body Wellness

We're dividing this section into two. I'm giving you practical tips on how to take care of your mental and physical wellness.

Mental Wellness

- Mindful breathing. Inhale for seven seconds, hold for four seconds, and exhale for another seven seconds. Repeat this breathing pattern for 10 minutes while you pay attention to how your chest expands and falls with each breath.

- Meditation. In a quiet room, close your eyes and start mindful breathing. While you do, scan your whole body, inch by inch, and identify points of tension. Try to clear your mind of any distractions and just focus on your breathing, your body, and the sensations you currently feel. You can also meditate on a thought or an intention, like what you want to accomplish (if you're meditating in the morning) or what you've accomplished (if you're meditating at night) for the day.

- Journaling. Writing your thoughts in a journal is one of the healthiest things you can do for your mind. You're able to process not just your thoughts but also your emotions. It also allows you to keep track of your state of mind and mental health progress, especially if you've been diagnosed with depression, anxiety, PTSD, and/or other mental health disorders.

- Self-care day. Allocate one day of the week for rest and relaxation. You can light some candles and have a glass of wine while you take a long bubble bath. Listen to soothing music. Deep condition your hair. Put on a face mask. Paint your nails. Whatever you need to unwind, do it. (Get more tips on how to find time for yourself in [Chapter 10](#).)

- Hobbies. Spend at least an hour out of a week doing something you love, whether that's baking, painting, calligraphy, puzzles, knitting, etc. A creative activity can take your mind off your current stressors and stimulate the right hemisphere of your brain.

Physical Wellness

- Yoga. Yoga is not only an exercise for the body—it is good for your mind too. It increases your flexibility, muscle strength, and metabolism. It can aid in weight loss, improve your cardiovascular health and athletic performance, and tone your muscles. In addition, it relieves chronic stress patterns, improves attention span, and sharpens concentration. It also brings calmness and increases body awareness during practice.

- Exercise. You can go to the gym. You can jog around the neighborhood. You can go for a hike. You can join a Zumba class. You can do CrossFit. It is up to you to choose which form of exercise is best for your fitness goals. The key here is to exercise regularly. Don't let a day pass by that you don't exercise. It doesn't always have to be an intense workout—walking home instead of taking the bus or using a standing desk instead of sitting all day are simple exercises you can do every day.

- Stretch. Don't take stretching for granted. Taking a short stretch break every half an hour can prevent tension from building in your back and shoulders, especially if you work at a desk for most of the day. Like yoga, stretching can improve your flexibility. It also improves your range of motion and posture, decreases tension headaches, and calms your mind.

- Sleep. Get a good night's sleep so you can recharge both your mind and body for the day ahead. You should have seven to nine hours of sleep every night. You can track your sleeping hours to see if you're getting enough using an app. (More on this in [Chapter 13](#).)

- Water. Make sure that you get enough water throughout the day. It is literally the simplest step that you can take to improve your physical wellness. On a daily basis, you need eight eight-ounce glasses of water (about two liters or half a gallon) to stay hydrated. To make it easier for you to track your water intake, invest in a one-liter water bottle that you can fill up twice a day.

Your Quick-Start Action Step: Choose at least one strategy each for mind and body wellness and include them in your schedule this week. Remember that these two facets work in tandem, so you need to cultivate them at the same time. For example, you can practice meditation every morning and make an effort to drink at least eight glasses of water every day. These are quick and easy steps that won't take too much of your time or energy.

Chapter 6: Dealing and Relieving Stress in the Workplace

Chapter 6: Dealing and Relieving Stress in the Workplace

We've all gone to work feeling uninspired. I'm sure that you've sat at your desk, staring at your computer screen and wishing that you could be anywhere but at the office. You've barely made a dent in the mountain of tasks that you need to finish before the day ends. The minutes are ticking by so slowly—every minute feels like forever.

Stress is an effective demotivator. Even those who love their job go through phases of indifference or apathy at work. It's completely normal to feel burnout, but it shouldn't be your normal state. After all, if stress is killing your drive, it's more challenging to achieve success.

In this chapter, we will talk about workplace stress and how to deal with it. I will give you useful tips on how to relieve stress at work so that you can do your job to the best of your abilities.

6.1 Stress in the Workplace

To truly understand stress in the workplace, we should first look into what a healthy working environment looks like.

A healthy working environment is where:

- leadership provides support to every member of the team,
- pressure is proportional to someone's abilities and resources,
- interpersonal relationships focus on teamwork and encouragement, and
- management and business practices promote healthy behaviors.

A healthy working environment should also provide fair compensation and benefits to workers. In addition, workers must be free from coercion, have job security, and be treated with respect and dignity at work.

When these conditions are not present in your place of work, stress is inevitable. Heavy workloads, people issues, juggling work and personal lives, and lack of job security are among the leading causes of workplace stress.

Stress in the workplace is also caused by the contents and context of the job. Let's discuss what each of these hazards mean.

Work Content Stressors

Work content stressors include job content, work pace, workload, working hours, and participation and control. To elaborate, stress can surface if:

- a person is not challenged by the job content (monotony, meaninglessness and lack of variety of tasks, under-stimulation);

- the deadline is not proportional to the amount of work (time pressure);

- the workload is not proportional to a person's abilities (too many tasks, not enough responsibilities);

- the working hours take time away from other roles (strict or inflexible schedule, long or unpredictable shifts); and

- a person has no control over decision making and other work processes.

Work Context Stressors

Work context stressors include career development, status and pay; organizational role; organizational culture; interpersonal relationships; and work-life balance. To elaborate, stress can surface if:

- a person has no room for career development, clear status in the company, or enough compensation (job insecurity, vague performance evaluation systems, no promotion opportunities);

- a person has an unclear role or there are conflicting roles in the organization;

- the organizational culture is toxic (unclear organizational objectives, poor leadership, lack of communication);

- interpersonal relationships at work are toxic (work harassment, unsupportive leadership, solitary work); and

- there is not enough work-life balance.

Aside from these stressors, people who are "stuck" in jobs that they're not passionate about also struggle with extreme stress. Even if the working environment provides ample support, the lack of passion will lead to negative emotions (sadness, cynicism, longing for "something better" or chasing "the dream") that can cause stress.

6.2 Effects of Workplace Stress

Workplace stress can have detrimental effects not just on your work performance but also on other aspects of your life. It can negatively affect your personal relationships and cognitive abilities. It can make you impatient and easily frustrated. It can also lead to sleepless nights, which will be bad for your mental and physical health.

On the other side of the coin, if you're the boss, stress in the workplace can create a ripple effect that your employees will suffer from. Worse, stress can make you an ineffective leader.

To avoid these problems, you need to find a healthy

coping mechanism for workplace stress. In addition, addressing workplace stress also:

- increases productivity,
- inspires creativity,
- reduces absences,
- improves efficiency, and
- leads to a positive attitude.

And if you're a happy worker/boss, you can motivate the people around you to have the same attitude towards work.

6.3 Managing Workplace Stress

The biggest challenge with workplace stress is that you rarely have control over your stressors. As an employee, you have business processes to follow, an organizational role to fill, and a manager or a boss to answer to. Sure, you can ask to be transferred to another shift if you're not happy with your schedule or to have more responsibilities if you're under-simulated at work, but your boss gets to make the final decision about these things.

If you own a business, you get to have more control over business processes, but you can't be sure that everything will run smoothly under your watch. Employees are prone to human error. Manufacturing and deliveries can be delayed. Customer demands and satisfaction can vary. There are a lot of factors that you need to keep an eye on to ensure your business success.

The best way to manage workplace stress is to have a coping strategy in place so that you can relieve stress even if you have little to no control over your stressors. It will vary from person to person depending on the demands of someone's job. But I am going to give you a list of things that you can use to create your own coping strategy.

Here are 10 techniques to relieve stress in the workplace:

- Get up and move throughout the day, especially if you work in an office. Stagnation can be bad for both your physical and mental health. Movement, on the other hand, stimulates your brain and rouses your body. So, take a short walk around the office, stretch, or get a cup of coffee.

- Decorate your office or cubicle with photos, mementos, and other similar objects that make you happy. Visual stimulation produces serotonin, the happy hormone, which can give you a boost of energy when you're starting to run low.

- Light a scented candle or use an essential oil diffuser. Peppermint, eucalyptus, and cardamom essential oils bring calmness. Meanwhile, citrus essential oils like orange, lemon, and grapefruit uplift your energy level and mood. (We'll talk about essential oils and their benefits in more detail later on in Chapter 10.)

- Spritz a rejuvenating facial spray when you need to feel more awake and energized.

- Perform short meditation exercises throughout the day. A five-minute guided meditation will bring you clarity and peace of mind. You can find meditation guides on YouTube.

- Take a snack break. Crunchy food items (like an apple or a trail mix) can wake you up when you feel sleepy at work.

- If your office has a garden or a similar outdoor space, go out and enjoy the scenery. Staring at your computer screen all day can cause eye strain and migraines. You need to take a five-minute break every half hour or so.

- Avoid procrastination. Try to always stay on top of your tasks instead of always chasing deadlines. Here are some actionable steps on how you can break this bad habit:

    - Get organized. At the start of each day, write a list of tasks that you need to accomplish. Use the prioritization technique that I taught you in Chapter 1 and plan your day accordingly.

    - Set achievable goals for yourself. You can't complete all of your important tasks for the week in one day, so get to the more urgent tasks first. This is why you need to implement my prioritization technique—it helps you streamline your tasks and avoid feeling overwhelmed.

- Create a daily schedule. For instance, you can finish all Level 1 tasks before lunch break, then move on to Level 2 tasks and work on them for the next two hours, and then move on to Level 3 tasks and work on them for the rest of the day. If you have Level 4 tasks at work, you can focus on them when you have time left before the day ends. (Remember that Level 4 tasks are not important and not urgent, so you may not even have them at the office.)

- Use incentives as a positive reinforcement. For instance, you can take a coffee break once you've returned all the emails in your inbox. You can get a snack once you've finished making the presentation for your client meeting. If you have these things to look forward to, you'll feel more motivated to finish your tasks.

- Recognize your hard work, even if the people at your job don't. Celebrate your own victories especially when you know that you did your best for a project.

- If your stressor involves bullying or harassment at work, report it to the human resources department immediately. As women, we are at a higher risk of experiencing sexual harassment and discrimination at work. You have to know your worth and realize that you don't need to endure these challenges to be able to do your job. You are capable, hardworking, and skilled. These qualities are the reason that you got the job. If someone makes you feel that you have to do things that are beyond your organizational role, that person is wrong and must be held accountable for inappropriate behavior.

Your Quick-Start Action Step: Create a quick stress-relief strategy that you can do at work. You can use a five-step sensory stimulation that involves looking at something that makes you happy, smelling a scented candle, wearing a soft cardigan, eating a crunchy snack, and listening to calming music.

Chapter 7: Dealing and Relieving Stress at Home

Chapter 7: Dealing and Relieving Stress at Home

Superman is a caped superhero who came to Earth from the planet Krypton via a spacecraft. When someone needs his help, he peels off his normal clothing to reveal his red and blue latex suit with the iconic S on the chest.

Superwoman, on the other hand, is the average woman. She looks just like you and me. She balances domestic responsibilities with her career. And just like Clark Kent, society doesn't know all of the superhero things that women are doing on a daily basis.

Sadly, the idea of "superwoman" is not as super as we may think. Most women will have to fill multiple roles in order to be considered adequate in our modern society. Even if we have more responsibilities than the average man, both at home and at work, society looks at us as if we're Clark Kent and shrugs. Society is also more observant of our flaws and incompetencies than our abilities and achievements.

As a result, we tend to be performative, i.e., to do things in pursuit of validation. It's a common experience for women to prove our worth. For them to take notice, we have to do more, be more, and be *really* super. We have to overachieve.

So, if you're a working mom, you have to be involved in the community too. Do charity work. Maybe build houses for the needy in your spare time. How about donate a kidney to show them that we are as altruistic as Superman? Even though it isn't fair for us to face this kind of pressure, it is the reality for most women.

In this chapter, we will discuss stress at home, keeping in mind that most women have multiple roles to fill. What can we do to manage home-related stressors so that we can continue excelling in other aspects of our lives?

7.1 Stress at Home

On average, working women report higher stress levels at home than working men, citing two primary reasons: the spilling effect of work and lower job satisfaction.

Work has a tendency to spill over at home because individuals don't have enough time at the office to finish all of their tasks. Since women are also expected to carry out domestic responsibilities such as child and home care, the spilling effect of work brings more stress at home for working women than working men.

At the same time, women report lower job satisfaction rates than men because we are underappreciated, underrepresented, and undercompensated in most industries.

- Underappreciation means we are often not given a proportional amount of responsibilities based on our abilities. More challenging and fulfilling roles are given to men. Men are also more likely to be promoted than women because 83.5% of executive positions are held by men, and men are more likely to promote other men than women.

- Underrepresentation means most industries are still male dominated. Without more women in our line of work, we face more pressure to overachieve because we want to prove that we earned our position.

- Undercompensation means we are not paid equally for the same job as men. On a global scale, women are paid 63% of what men are paid. The World Economic Forum predicts that it will take the world 202 years to close the gender pay gap.

I know that this chapter should be about stressors that women face at home. However, we have to talk about these job-related pressures to understand why women are more stressed at home than men. We have to work twice as hard as men just to get ahead in our careers, which we often do by taking work home with us. Even when we're not in the office, we're still thinking about work. And then, when we go to work, we're still thinking about our children and our tasks at home.

Women who don't have children also face a lot of pressure in terms of their home life. Because society expects women to be married and have children at a certain age to be considered normal, some of those who don't want to conform to these traditional gender expectations use their jobs and accolades to compensate for what they "lack" in life. Even without families, we still have to prove our worth and show people that we are enough. We are adequate. We may not fit what society thinks is ideal, but we send a message that we only need ourselves to obtain achievements and live fulfilled lives.

Home is also where we spend time with our families, invite friends over and socialize, and think about basic needs, mortgage payments, and utilities. Most of our important roles are performed at home: wife, mother, daughter, friend, etc. In other words, the pressure of accomplishing multiple roles is felt at home the most. It becomes a hub where multiple stressors intersect.

7.2 Effects of Stress at Home

An effective coping strategy for home-related stress will help us prevent its negative effects including the following:

- We've established that the home is where we perform our most important roles. Therefore, if we feel stress at home, it affects our ability to fulfill our duties to the best of our abilities.

- Stress at home can cause a ripple effect that those who live with us feel. This ripple effect is

- particularly difficult for children who have yet to understand what stress does to a person's mind and body.

- Home is sanctuary for most of us. It is where we rest and recharge. When our homes are filled with stress, we lose our sacred space.

In addition, dealing with stress at home will:

- strengthen personal relationships with family members,

- positively influence younger generations,

- create a supportive and loving environment,

- improve overall outlook in life, and

- lead to long-term happiness and contentment.

7.3 Managing Stress at Home

Unlike stress in the workplace, you have more control about stress at home because you are one of the leaders of the household. However, an effective coping strategy will still vary depending on your current situation and the different responsibilities that you have. I'm going to give you some practical tips on how to manage stress at home, no matter who you are. Here are 12 techniques that you can easily apply:

- Delegate chores. You shouldn't be the only one in your family who looks after the house. After all, you're not the only resident of the house. You can put up a whiteboard in the common area (like the living room, kitchen, or dining room) where you can write the names of each member of the household along with their corresponding chores for the week. (You can also use this system to keep track of everyone's most important activities for the week.)

- Do not work in the bedroom. You should only associate this room with rest and relaxation. Otherwise, your brain will associate it with work, alertness, and adrenaline, which can negatively affect your sleeping cycle.

- Spend at least one hour each day with your family. No matter how busy everyone is, don't take quality family time for granted.

- Create a personal space where you can meditate and unwind after a particularly stressful day. (You can find more tips about personal spaces in [Chapter 11](#).)

- Cultivate an open line of communication with your family members. You should be able to tell them when you need quiet time by yourself and vice versa.

- Avoid bringing home too much work. Your house is not an extension of your office. Don't let work take over your sanctuary.

- Keep your house as organized as possible. Clutter is the most common stressor in the home. You can use bins and baskets to hide objects in. Put labels on each container so that everyone in your house knows what to use it for.

- Address issues with your family members as soon as possible. Settle arguments by talking in a productive, understanding, and supportive manner.

- Accept that you can't control everything. Trying will only lead to stress. Go back to the Serenity Prayer and say it to yourself like a mantra if you must.

- Take note of your due dates for mortgage payments, bills, and other utilities. Financial problems are the biggest stressor for a lot of people. To avoid paying high interest rates, make sure that you settle these payables on time.

- Allocate one day out of the week for work-free fun with your family or friends.

- Learn to say no. You don't need to accept more responsibilities, especially if your plate is already full. Overworking yourself will lead to fatigue and more stress.

Your Quick-Start Action Step: To relieve stress quickly at home, seek refuge in your personal space. Even a half hour alone can completely change your mood. You can take a bath, meditate, or practice yoga during this time. You can also create a playlist of songs that instantly calms you down so that you can listen to it when your day is packed with chores and other activities.

Chapter 8: Quick Stress Management Techniques you can Apply

Chapter 8: Quick Stress Management Techniques You Can Apply

The previous three chapters focused on detailed stress coping strategies that you need to work on and slowly incorporate into your daily habits. It may take some time before you are able to apply them as a normal part of your life. While you're integrating these techniques to break bad behaviors that lead to chronic stress, acute stressors can still materialize. On some days, you'll have a hectic schedule. On others, you'll feel stressed even if you don't have a lot of tasks on your list. But it gets really bad when you are both busy and stressed. In times like these, what do you do?

This chapter will focus on quick stress management techniques for when you simply have no time to stress about, well, stress. The tips that I will share with you in the last section of this chapter can be done between one and three minutes—yes, they're *that* fast and easy. And yes, they are effective.

For a quick pick-me-up during a particularly difficult day, keep reading this chapter.

8.1 Instantly Stress Free

Instant coffee. Instant messaging. Instant delivery. As our world becomes more and more fast paced, different industries have come up with different types of instant goods and services. You can order something online and have it on your doorstep the very next day. You don't even need to leave the house when you need something from the store. Tap, tap, tap and voila! We can literally live comfortable lives without having to step outside our homes.

However, even though technological and scientific advancements have made all of these possible, we are still human. We don't operate like robots. When stressors are present, we need to process them at our own pace and deal with their negative effects using coping mechanisms because we are sentient beings. You can't push a button or tap a screen to remove stress instantly. (You can use apps to help manage stress though. More on this later on.)

In recent years, stress levels around the world have been increasing steadily. In 2018, more than one in three adults reported to have experienced a lot of stress and worry. As a result, at least three in 10 adults reported to have experienced physical pain while one in five adults experienced sadness or anger. This survey was conducted in 142 countries around the world. It is apparent from these survey results that life has become more challenging as our world becomes more modern.

When demands and stress are increasing rapidly, what can we do to maintain overall wellness?

The first thing you need to change is your unproductive habits. To do so, you can use the techniques that I taught you in the earlier chapters. However, like I mentioned earlier, it takes some getting used to before you can fully adopt them into your daily life. While you're making fundamental changes, you need a quick stress management strategy in place.

8.2 Benefits of Quick Stress Management Techniques

A quick stress management strategy focuses on dealing and relieving acute stress that comes from day-to-day challenges, like if you woke up late or if your car broke down. With it in place, you will be able to:

- calmly handle unforeseen obstacles,
- get back on track in terms of time,
- move on from acute stressors and finish the rest of your tasks,
- solve problems with a level head,
- avoid adding fuel to your chronic stress, if you have any, and
- keep a positive attitude throughout the day.

Think about stress as a scrape. A comprehensive stress management strategy is your body that heals the wound from the inside. The scrape may not disappear overnight, but you know that your body is doing its job. To help protect yourself from wound infections (or cumulative stress), you put a bandage (or implement a quick stress management strategy) over it. Put a few extra bandages in your purse so that you can reach for them any time.

8.3 Quick Stress Management Techniques

A quick stress management strategy involves mini-relaxation exercises that help burst stress bubbles that come to the surface throughout the day. You can perform them at the office, in your car while you're stuck in traffic, or while waiting at the doctor's office—basically any place where you might encounter acute stressors.

I am going to teach you three mini-relaxation exercises for when you have a minute, two, or three. And I want you to try them out as you read, starting with the longest quick stress management technique.

Three Minutes

Set a timer for 180 seconds on your phone before we begin. Ready? Great. Start the timer.

1. Find a comfortable position and then close your eyes. (You can keep your eyes open if this is your first time doing this mini-relaxation exercise so you can continue reading the instructions.) Identify the situation that is causing you stress at the moment.

2. Ask yourself: Is this something that I can control? If you answered no, skip to step 4. If you answered yes, proceed to step 3.

3. What three things can you do to address the situation? Create a list in your head. For instance, you can prepare for an upcoming test by turning off your phone, focusing on your study materials, and taking a practice test.

4. If there's nothing you can do about the stressor (like if your train is late) or if you've identified three productive steps to address it, I want you to start counting from 10. With each even number, breathe in. With each odd number, breathe out. Continue doing this until you reach 1.

5. Repeat the previous step as needed.

6. Take another deep breath. This time, I want you to smile slowly as you inhale. You should be fully smiling as you breathe out.

Two Minutes

Now set a timer for 120 seconds. Hit start and let's

begin.

1. In the first 10 seconds of this exercise, I want you to scan your body for points of tension. Start from the top of your head to the bottom of your feet. Did you find them? You can find tension in your facial muscles, shoulders, arms, etc.

2. Now that you've identified these points of tension, move around to engage these muscle groups. Then relax your muscles and release the tension from them. For instance, you can open and close your jaw, roll your shoulders front to back, and shake your arms. Then close your mouth, drop your shoulders, and rest your arms on your lap with fingers spread apart.

3. In the last 90 seconds, I want you to do mindful breathing. Close your eyes and focus on every breath you take. One cycle of mindful breathing will take 18 seconds. You'll be able to do about five cycles during this exercise.

One Minute

If you've been doing the last two exercises as you read

them, you should be feeling less stressed by now. Do you feel better? Amazing!

For our last exercise, set the timer for 60 seconds. Done? This is the simplest quick stress management technique so let's jump right in. Start the clock.

1. Lie down if you can. If not, sitting is fine too. Like the first two techniques, I want you to close your eyes.

2. Now, follow "countdown from 10" breathing technique that I taught you earlier. Breathe in slowly on even numbers and breathe out on odd numbers. It's important that you count in your head while you breathe so you can shift your focus away from the stressor.

3. After doing one cycle, start again from 10. This time, I want you to say "I am" before breathing in on even numbers and "at peace" before breathing out on odd numbers. You can change the second phrase to "capable," "going to be fine," or "doing great," whatever fits your current situation.

4. Take another deep breath and smile slowly as you inhale. Release the last breath with a sigh.

Your Quick-Start Action Step: Choose one from these quick stress management techniques (whatever is appropriate for the situation), and apply it the next time you encounter an acute stressor.

Chapter 9: Managing Stress in a Relationship

Chapter 9: Managing Stress in a Relationship

In this chapter, I will give you tips on how to manage stress in a relationship. To be exact, we will be talking about romantic relationships. This chapter is for those who are dating or married. But even if you're currently unattached, you should keep reading because you may find some tips that you can apply in other types of relationships, like friendships or professional affiliations.

Before proceeding to our conversation, I first want to ask you a couple of questions. You can also ask your partner these questions when you're ready to work on the stressors in your relationship together.

1. What is your biggest stressor at the moment?
2. Does it involve your partner? If yes, how can you find resolution? If not, does it spillover to your relationship?
3. Are you currently in conflict with your partner? What caused the fight?

4. If you answered yes to the last question, is it your fault? What can you do to apologize? If not, can you work on forgiveness?

5. If you answered no to the third question, how can your partner help you relieve stress?

6. Is there anything you can personally do to manage your own stress?

7. What activities can you do together to relieve stress?

8. Do you need time alone? If yes, how can you convey it to your partner without hurting their feelings?

These questions will help you determine if stress is present in your relationship and whether it is brought about by the relationship or by external factors. Once you've answered these questions, you're ready to learn more about relationship stress and how to better manage it.

9.1 Relationship Stress

The causality of stress in a relationship can be reciprocal. As I see it, stress can bring problems into a relationship and problems in a relationship can cause stress. Let's talk about the latter by looking at some of the most common sources of stress in relationships:

- uncertainty
- power imbalance
- lack of independence
- lack of safety
- miscommunication
- manipulation

When you're uncertain about your relationship, you wonder about its longevity or whether your partner likes you or not. (I'm sure that most of you know that it's possible to love someone and dislike them at the same time.) If you're questioning these aspects of your relationship, you can become very insecure, which can result in jealousy, an unhealthy attachment, and/or trust issues.

When there is a power imbalance in the relationship,

one is more dominant than the other. The more dominant partner will have more say on where the relationship is going. They can decide on things like which friends the more passive partner can hang out with or where they will go on vacations. It is also possible for two people to engage in a power tug-of-war; they both want to win in the relationship, whether that's by defeating the other in an argument or by getting to make the decisions. Being challenged in a relationship can be healthy to some degree, but too much conflict will result in displeasure, discontent, and bitterness.

Even though you're in a relationship, you should still have independence. What this means is that you need to have an identity outside the relationship. When you lose your identity, your self-worth will decline. You will start to look for validation from your partner, and your confidence will depend on how they are treating you. It can be exhausting for your partner to have this responsibility. Worse, you may open yourself to risks because the wrong person will take advantage of your lack of independence.

In addition, safety, trust, and respect are very

important in a relationship. If your partner exhibits behaviors that make you feel emotionally, physically, and/or financially unsafe, you should seriously think about whether you should be with this person or not.

A lack of communication or misunderstanding can cause a lot of stress in a relationship. When one or both parties refuse to open up about their real feelings, they create a gap that can become unbridgeable if not resolved immediately.

Manipulation happens when one person lies or deceives the other to get what they want. It can put trust on the line. In fact, it can put the whole relationship on the line.

These are seven of the most common relationship stressors. Like I said earlier, external stressors can also cause problems in the relationship. Work, for example, easily spills over to the relationship, especially when one or both parties are career driven. Home stress, like unequal domestic responsibilities, can also seep into the relationship.

9.2 Effects of Relationship Stress

As if the aforementioned relationship stressors aren't bad enough on their own, they can create more problems in the relationship. Here are a few examples of how relationship stress can affect you and your partner:

- It can make simple arguments much worse.
- It can prevent one or both parties from growing as individuals.
- It can prevent the relationship itself from growing and moving forward.
- It can affect your performance at work and other responsibilities.
- Extreme relationship stress can cause psychological trauma.
- Partners who have external stressors can get trapped in a cycle of catching each other's stress.
- Resentment can stem from uncertainty, power imbalance, lack of independence, lack of security, miscommunication, and/or

manipulation. In a lot of relationships, resentment is the straw that breaks the camel's back.

Knowing the negative effects of relationship stress, I think you can see why you should address it as soon as you recognize that it exists. In addition, managing relationship stress will also:

- create a stronger bond between you and your partner,
- lead to a more open line of communication,
- strengthen trust in each other,
- cultivate respect for one another,
- build a safe and supportive environment for both parties,
- improve sex life and intimacy, and
- increase overall happiness and satisfaction in the relationship.

9.3 Managing Stress in a Relationship

To help you achieve all of the wonderful benefits that I mentioned above, I want to share with you a few thoughts that you can reflect on if you want to change your perspective about your relationship. You can turn these ideas into a mindset so that you can better manage relationship stress in the future.

- Do not shove problems under the rug. When there is an issue, talk about it as soon as possible. When you ignore problems, you're not escaping them. All you're doing is creating a pile of issues that can come crashing down at any minute.

- Avoid talking about your problems in public. Find a place where you both feel safe and discuss the source of stress in your relationship. You can ask each other the questions that I listed at the beginning of this chapter.

- When you're ready to sit down and talk about your issues, be honest about the things that bother you but express yourself in a compassionate manner. In Chapter 4, I mentioned how you should avoid accusations, i.e., "You did this. You said that." Instead, convey your emotions and say, "I felt…"

- When it's your partner's turn to talk about their feelings and/or issues, listen. And don't just hear the words that are coming out of their mouth—let them sink in. Try to look at the problem from their point of view.

- You need to realize that a relationship is a partnership. It's always you and your partner against the problem, not against each other. When you win, you both win. When you lose, you both lose.

- Spend some quality time…alone. You need to maintain your sense of independence no matter how long you've been in a relationship with your partner. Don't be afraid to ask for space when you need to. After all, how can you love someone else if you don't love yourself first and foremost?

Aside from these tips, you should also foster and maintain intimacy by doing a few or all of the following:

- Talk about each other's day.

- Start a hobby together, like going on a jog or playing board games.

- Go on a date at least once a week. (Netflix and chill don't count—get dressed, go out, and have a fun time.)

- Take a vacation together at least once a year.

- Settle huge arguments before you sleep at night. Don't let them fester.

- Hug more often.

- Kiss each other good night.

- Say "I love you" at least once every day.

Your Quick-Start Action Step: Answer the questions at the beginning of the chapter. If there is a pressing issue that you need to address, schedule a sit-down talk with your partner right away.

You should also choose at least two of the intimacy

tips above and turn them into a habit.

Chapter 10: Finding Time for Yourself

Chapter 10: Finding Time for Yourself

In earlier chapters, I talked about how stress can lead people to escape in isolation, which can then develop into mental health problems like anxiety and depression. Under extreme stress, people can be compelled to separate themselves from their friends, family, and the rest of the world. This type of isolation is detrimental to a person's overall wellness. It can cause feelings of helplessness and hopelessness.

When I say that you need alone time every once in a while, I don't mean isolation. The difference between the two is that the former is a momentary period of self-reflection and rejuvenation while the latter is an extended period of solitude and despondency. The former is good for your mental health while the latter leads to more complicated problems.

In this chapter, we will focus on finding time for yourself. We will talk about why spending time alone is good for you and how it can help alleviate stress and its symptoms. We will also discuss how you can avoid having feelings of guilt whenever you want time for yourself. At the end of the chapter, I will give you a list of things that you can do to refresh your mind and body during your alone time.

10.1 Alone Time

Putting this concept in the simplest terms, alone time pertains to time that you spend away from other people. It is a time for rest, relaxation, and reflection, but it can also be your time to do activities that contribute to your physical well-being. As much as possible, you need to include it in your regular schedule. I suggest you have alone time during the weekend so that you can feel refreshed at the start of a new week.

You should also have alone time when you're starting to feel burned out. Keep an eye out for these warning signs:

1. You have lost interest in things that you used to find fulfilling or entertaining.

2. You can't seem to find joy in whatever you do.

3. You find it hard to stay motivated, inspired, and/or creative.

4. You have no drive to complete mundane everyday tasks.

5. You have been cancelling a lot of social plans so you can stay at home in isolation.

6. You have been exhibiting addictive behaviors such as binge-eating and/or drug and alcohol abuse.

7. You get overwhelmed by the smallest things.

8. You get annoyed by the simplest inconveniences.

9. You have been transferring stress onto other people.

10. Your stress is starting to negatively affect your relationship with other people.

11. You can't focus on tasks no matter how urgent or important they are.

12. Your anxiety level is not proportional to your situation.

13. You've been experiencing a lot of physical pain like migraines, aching muscles, and digestion problems.

14. Your energy level is always running on low even after a full night of sleep.

15. You have developed thoughts of self-loathing and/or self-pity.

Have you noticed one or more of these warning signs in yourself? If yes, then you need to hit the restart button and spend some alone time with yourself.

10.2 Guilt-Free Alone Time

Most women I know associate alone time with feelings of guilt. Because of our multiple roles, we feel like we have no time for self-care. We'd rather spend our time on more "productive" activities like work or chores. Society also expects us to prioritize other people over ourselves. Women are perceived as nurturers and caretakers.

Therefore, when we prioritize ourselves, we feel like we're stepping out of line and not performing to standard. We worry about what society will say about us if, God forbid, we spend an hour or two every week taking care of ourselves instead of others.

To remove these feelings of guilt when you need alone time, focus on its benefits and how it can help you become a better version of yourself. In my opinion, there are 10 great benefits to having a dedicated alone time. It will help you to:

- build mental strength,
- increase happiness level,
- improve life satisfaction,
- create an opportunity to reflect on your life purpose,
- boost energy levels,
- develop problem-solving skills,
- refresh creativity and concentration,
- reinforce positive self-image,

- process both chronic and acute stressors and identify ways to cope, and

- rejuvenate overall mental and physical state.

If alone time gives you these great personal benefits, you will be able to fulfill your responsibilities more effectively. In retrospect, it doesn't just make you feel better—it also allows you to excel in your different roles so that you can achieve success in all areas. So why should you feel guilty about it?

Moreover, you deserve to take a break once in a while. There's nothing wrong about taking care of yourself especially when you work so hard. Don't let what others may say about you make you feel less deserving.

10.3 Things to Do during Your Alone Time

When you spend some quality alone time, I don't want you to just sit around in your sweatpants and watch TV all day. Take note of one important word: quality. Whatever you do during your alone time, it should have a positive effect on your physical and/or mental wellness. Otherwise, you're just spending a day in isolation, which is what we want to avoid.

So, I'm going to give you a few ideas on what you can do during your alone time. These are things that I personally do when I need to be by myself:

- Read a book. Fiction novels may stimulate creativity and give you an opportunity to escape real-world problems so that you can come back with a fresh perspective. When it comes to nonfiction books, I recommend reading the autobiographies of your favorite celebrities. You will be inspired by how they were able to overcome difficult situations in their own lives and achieve success. My personal favorites include:

    - *Becoming* by Michelle Obama (Former First Lady of the United States)

    - *Yes Please* by Amy Poehler (Actress and Comedian)

    - *Bossypants* by Tina Fey (Actress and Comedian)

- *Scrappy Little Nobody* by Anna Kendrick (Actress)

- *Is Everyone Hanging Out Without Me? (And Other Concerns)* by Mindy Kaling (Actress)

- *Talking as Fast as I can* by Lauren Graham (Actress)

- *Courage to Soar* by Simone Biles (Gymnast and Olympic Gold Medalist)

- *Year of Yes* by Shonda Rhimes (Producer and Writer)

- *The Last Black Unicorn* by Tiffany Haddish (Actress and Comedian)

- *This Will Only Hurt a Little* by Busy Philipps (Actress)

- Work out. Physical exercises can also be meditative. Yoga, hiking, and jogging can strengthen your body and relax your mind, especially if you have a beautiful view while exercising. I highly recommend working out outdoors instead of going to the gym.

- Take a long bath. The warm water will soothe your aching muscles. The smell of your bath products will calm your senses. You can also light candles, listen to an audiobook about wellness and self-care, and put on a face mask while taking a bath. Aside from using this time to unwind, you can also use products that nourish your skin.

- When you have more time, go to a spa or salon and get pampered. Get a massage, get your nails done, or get a facial. Treating yourself once in a while is not frivolous. If it makes you feel good about yourself and contributes to your overall wellness, then it's an investment towards your health.

- Dance. Play your favorite tunes, get up, and move. Dancing releases adrenaline and happy hormones that can instantly bring up your mood. Not to mention, dancing is also a fun way of exercising.

- If you have a journal, list down all of the things that you are grateful for. Taking a moment to recognize all the good things in your life will change your outlook. You will have a more positive attitude. This exercise will also help you put stress in perspective. How does it compare to your achievements? Don't you have more things to be grateful for?

- If you enjoy driving, go on a road trip. Don't plan an itinerary—just go. See where your heart leads you. Play your favorite songs while you drive and just enjoy the ride. I find this particularly relaxing. When I'm feeling overwhelmed, I go on a short ride and maybe grab some ice cream on my way home. It's the simple things in life that really bring me out of a funk.

- Spend time in nature and let its healing powers restore you. There's a reason why people like to take vacations in nature. One, you can escape the hustle and bustle of the city. And two, being surrounded by nature is therapeutic. But you don't need to plan a whole trip just to get away.

Take an afternoon walk if you live close to the beach or sit outside if you have a garden and breathe some fresh air.

You can also watch a movie or binge the latest episodes of your favorite TV show during your alone time, but it shouldn't be the only thing that you do. Again, if it doesn't benefit your physical or mental health, it does not bring any quality into your life, which defeats the purpose of alone time.

Your Quick-Start Action Step: Look at your weekly schedule and allot at least two hours for your alone time. Two hours is just 1.19% of your entire week (or 1.79% excluding sleeping hours, given that you get eight hours of sleep every night.) The time you spend alone barely makes a dent in your schedule so you can't use "busy" as an excuse to avoid it. Then choose one self-care tip from the list that I gave you in the previous section and try to turn it into a habit.

Chapter 11: Taking Opportunities to Recharge

Chapter 11: Taking Opportunities to Recharge

Except for a slight dip after the 2008 global financial crisis, the international tourism industry has steadily experienced growth. In 2007, there were more than 920 million international arrivals. After 10 years, the latest available data show that there were more than 1.341 billion international arrivals. That's a 421-million jump in the last 10 years. In 2017, 55% of tourists traveled for leisure, recreation, and holidays; 27% traveled to visit friends and relatives, for health reasons, and/or for religious reasons; and 13% traveled for business and professional reasons.

Based on international tourist arrivals, tourism revenues, and tourism growth, the top international destinations are:

With people becoming more interested in traveling and seeing more of the world, the international tourism industry has never been better. Tourism creates jobs, resulting in economic growth and development. In fact, the total contribution of travel and tourism to the global economy was $8.27 trillion in 2016. The global hotel industry's total retail value was $570.18 billion while the global online travel bookings revenue was $513 billion in the same year. Aside from economic growth and development, tourism also leads to cultural preservation, environmental protection, and peace and security.

So why am I talking about the tourism industry? Well, it's because I believe that for those who have means, traveling can have a significant positive impact to your overall wellness. I believe in the restorative benefits of vacations. They give you opportunities to recharge so that you can reduce both short-term and long-term stress.

In this chapter, I want to talk about taking vacations and how they can help you recharge your body and mind.

11.1 Recharging Your Body and Mind

There are so many things that you can do to recharge your body and mind right now. In the previous chapter, we discussed the importance of spending some quality time alone. I also gave you some ideas on how you can maximize your alone time so that you can feel refreshed at the start of every week. We've also talked about how you can deal with and relieve stress in the workplace and at home. The techniques I've taught you so far can be easily integrated into your daily life. In other words, you can make them a habit.

But when you feel drained, I believe that taking a vacation is also a great solution. Stress, especially chronic stress, can lead to burnout that prevents you from fulfilling your responsibilities to the best of your abilities. In Chapter 10, I gave you a list of warning signs that tell you when you're feeling burned out. You can also use them to determine whether you need a vacation or not. If you're experiencing several of these warning signs at once, then you deserve to get away for a while.

Of course, taking a vacation is not an instant solution like alone time is. You need to plan it carefully and to spend money on it. That's why it's important to have more habitual coping mechanisms in place so that you can relieve stress in real time. If alone time is like a bandage that you put over a wound, a vacation is like going to the hospital to get treatment for an illness that a bandage can't fix.

11.2 Importance of Recharging Your Body and Mind

In the context of recharging one's body and mind, I see five main reasons as to why people love to travel:

1. Traveling is a form of escape from the usual humdrum of people's lives. I've mentioned this earlier, but stepping away from your current situation to do something recreational allows you to gain a different perspective. As the saying goes, things look different from a distance. Traveling allows you to view your life from a wider angle. You become more grateful for the things that you have, and you're able to assess your stressors in relation to your blessings. You'll be able to see how hard you've been working to achieve your goals and to ultimately reach success.

2. Traveling opens the door to learning. When you visit a new place, you get to see a new way of living, gain new experiences, and meet new people. You get to see things that you haven't

seen before. Maybe eat food that you haven't tasted before. Hear new sounds and smell new scents. You get to learn about the history and culture of the place. You also get to learn more about yourself and how you adapt to a new environment. Traveling always involves stepping out of your comfort zone. Therefore, it can help you grow as a more confident version of yourself.

3. Traveling gives you time for a little rest and restoration. Hopefully, you're not thinking about work, domestic, and other responsibilities during your vacation. So, when you travel, you allow yourself to just be in the moment instead of chasing deadlines and ticking tasks off a checklist. You don't feel like you're running after your life. You do activities that make you happy or that excite you. Whether you're just lounging by the pool or following a full itinerary, you're getting a break from your usual stressors.

4. Traveling can improve your productivity. When you're always rushing to meet deadlines, you

run the risk of getting burned out. When this happens, you are unable to perform at your peak level. Because traveling gives you a break from work, you are also able to take a break from stressors and toxic behaviors that lead to burnout. There's a reason why most companies have mandatory leaves in place for their employees. Studies have shown that vacations actually improve a person's productivity when they return to the office.

5. Traveling can improve your quality of life. Studies have shown that vacations have cardiovascular health benefits. Women who take less time off work are almost eight times more likely to develop heart disease. Moreover, vacations also interrupt habits, like overworking and using a backlit screen before bed, that lead to sleeplessness. As a result, you will sleep better after a vacation.

11.3 From Drained to Rejuvenated

For some people, planning a trip is a stressor in itself. Just thinking about the logistics—choosing a destination, booking flights and accommodations, and creating an itinerary—seem like a lot of work. So, I want to give you a 12-item checklist to help you plan a trip that will transform you from drained to rejuvenated.

1. Destination

The first step in planning a trip is to choose a destination. What type of experience do you want to have? Are you taking a vacation simply for relaxation or do you want to have more of an adventure? Do you want to be surrounded by nature or visit a new city? What time of year are you planning to go on a trip? Seasons may also affect your decision.

When choosing a destination, take your budget and time into consideration as well. How much money are you willing to spend on this trip? How long can you be away from work and other responsibilities? You should also consider who you're traveling with. If you have young children, it might be hard to go somewhere too far.

2. Flight

Once you've chosen a destination, you can book a flight. I have found that there are three things you can do to cut the cost of your airfare. Here are my top tricks to booking cheaper flights:

- Search for flights in incognito mode on your web browser. If you've been researching about a specific destination, airline websites will use saved cookies to offer you higher prices. The incognito mode will hide those cookies so you can get base prices for plane tickets.

- Use a flight search engine that compares multiple airline websites at once so you can easily find the cheapest options.

- Use your airline miles or credit card rewards to get discounts and/or upgrades.

3. Accommodation

After booking your flight, you should book your accommodation next. You should look for hotels, motels, or Airbnbs in the area and find the option that has the best location and amenities for its cost. To determine which type of accommodation is most suited for the type of vacation that you're taking, I've compiled a list of considerations for each.

Hotels are a great option if you are:

- going on a vacation mostly for relaxation,
- not staying for too long at your destination, and
- traveling solo or with one to three people.

Motels are a great option if you:

- want to save money,
- are backpacking or don't have a lot of luggage, and
- have a fuller itinerary and just need a place to stay the night.

Airbnbs are a great option if you:

- are traveling with a large group of people,
- want to get the best value for money, and
- want to have complete privacy and freedom in the space.

4. Transportation

You need to think about how you'll get around once

you reach your destination. You should research about available public transportation and/or car rentals. Is walking an option? Maybe you can rent a bike if your stops are close to one another. If you're taking public transportation, you should also look into passes or access cards. Some cities around the world require all passengers to have them to be able to board. For island vacations, will you need to ride boats? Where are the ports? Can you book boat rides with tour packages?

5. Attractions

You can create a bucket list of attractions that you need to see during your vacation or, better yet, make an itinerary so you have a clearer idea of where you need to be on a specific time. For people who like structure, I suggest the latter. You can also look for a travel agency, so you won't have to worry about transportation and/or food during your tour. For budget travelers, you can find free things to do in the place you're visiting. There's a lot of information on the internet about places you can visit if you're working with a limited budget.

6. Cafés, Bars, and Restaurants

I believe that food is a huge part of the culture of any locality. You can learn a lot about a place's culture (and often history too) through its cuisine. So, I suggest that you also include cafés, bars, restaurants, and other places to eat at when you're planning a trip. Try beignets in New Orleans, deep dish pizza in Chicago, and ribs in Texan cities. Paris is known for its macarons and pastries, India is known for curry and spicy dishes, and Japan is known for sushi, ramen, and tempura. You can also find interesting dishes to try in markets and street carts in some countries. So, let your palate take you on another kind of adventure during your vacation.

7. Documents

Don't forget to prepare the necessary documents that you need for the trip. All overseas trips require you to have a passport so make sure that it won't expire before or during your vacation. If you don't have a passport yet, give yourself enough time to acquire one. Don't schedule your international trip if you're not sure that you're going to get your passport on time.

You should also look into visa requirements. Each country will have different rules for applications and types of visas that you can apply for. Double check on the embassy's website to make sure that you're applying for the right one and that you have all the requirements that you need in order to get approved.

Aside from your passport and visa, you should prepare other necessary documents like flight tickets, itineraries, hotel reservations, rental car reservations, tour confirmations, government-issued IDs, credit and/or debit cards, etc. For safekeeping and convenience, save a copy of your documents on your phone.

8. Travel Insurance

Most people don't purchase travel insurance for international trips. In fact, only 38% of American tourists are likely to purchase travel insurance.

I personally recommend that you buy travel insurance so that you can be protected when unforeseen circumstances occur. Travel insurance may cover cancellations due to personal reasons (like death in the family or illness) and cancelled flights due to airline problems, terrorist attacks, and natural disasters. It may also cover delayed or lost baggage, injuries acquired during the trip, medical emergencies, and lost passports.

9. Immunizations

Before you leave, do some research about health hazards at your destination. You may want to get immunizations so you can prevent getting sick. To determine what type of vaccination you need, consult with your primary care doctor at least two months before your departure.

10. Packing

Packing is probably one of the most stressful parts of planning a vacation. If you're like most people I know, you put it off until the very last minute and, by then, you're just throwing whatever you can into your suitcase. The problem with this is that you tend to forget important items that you need during the vacation. To prevent this problem, here are my five tips to packing efficiently:

- Create a checklist of everything you need to pack for the vacation and be as specific as possible. Clothes, shoes, gadgets, toiletries, makeup, and accessories are general categories. Here's a sample checklist:

- 5 shirts
- 2 jeans
- 2 shorts
- 3 swimsuits
- 2 dresses
- 5 pairs of underwear
- pajamas
- running shoes
- sandals
- flip flops
- soap
- shampoo
- toothpaste and toothbrush
- face wash
- moisturizer
- sunscreen
- lotion

• Pack according to your destination. If you're going on a tropical vacation, don't pack knitwear and thick jackets that take up space in your suitcase. You won't need them anyway. If you're going to a cold destination, plan your day-to-day outfits so you don't overpack. You can try out outfits before you leave and take a photo of each, so you know exactly what to wear during your vacation.

- Use packing cubes for smaller items like socks, intimates, and swimwear, so you won't have to dig through your suitcase to find them.

- You should have a pouch, preferably made of plastic or waterproof material, for your toiletries and makeup.

- Instead of folding your clothes, roll them into tubes so you can fit more in your suitcase.

11. Money

Make sure that you have enough pocket money (and a little extra in case of emergencies) for your trip. You don't need to carry cash (unless you're going somewhere remote) because I think it's safer if you use a debit or credit card. Just make sure to inform your credit card provider that you're going on a trip, especially if you're traveling far, so they won't freeze your card.

12. Online Check-in

Most airlines today accept online check-ins. A few days before your flight, you can use this feature, so you don't have to check-in at the airport hours before boarding. You'll get your boarding pass via email, which makes the process much easier.

Your Quick-Start Action Step: Plan your next vacation. Look at your calendar and find the perfect time to take a vacation. Don't worry about expenses or logistics—just create a bucket list of places that you want to visit and sights that you want to see. The key here is to take the first step in planning your next getaway, even if it's still months away.

Chapter 12: How to Avoid Mistakes when Dealing with Stress

Chapter 12: How to Avoid Mistakes when Dealing with Stress

You've probably already noticed this, but stress can actually cause more stress. For a lot of people, it's like pouring water over a burning pan. Because the pan is so hot, the water will just evaporate, and the oxygen from the water will stoke the flame. A professional chef will tell you to cover the pan with a lid. Doing so will suffocate the flame and extinguish it.

We sometimes think that we're doing the right thing to manage stress. Like pouring water over a burning pan, we make mistakes when dealing with stress and use the wrong strategies to cope. As a result, we stoke the flame. We make the problem worse.

So, how can you avoid making mistakes when dealing with stress? In this chapter, we will talk about common stress management mistakes and foolproof solutions to avoid them.

12.1 Why You Need to Avoid Stress Management Mistakes

Have you ever made a mistake and tried to fix it with

the wrong solution? Like putting too much fertilizer in the soil to save a dying plant—over-fertilization or fertilizer burn can cause root damage and kill the plant that you're trying to save. Perhaps you've tried to spruce up old furniture by repainting it, but you forgot to sand it first—the paint will not be able to cling onto the wood and will most likely chip after a while.

Sometimes our goal is to make something better, but our execution of the plan is riddled with mistakes. When this happens, the end product is usually worse than the starting point.

The same principle applies when you make stress management mistakes. Instead of alleviating stressors, you make them worse or add new ones into the equation. As a result, your acute stress turns into chronic stress. Your chronic stress turns into a mental health problem like anxiety or depression.

Therefore, you must avoid making mistakes when you manage stress. Aside from preventing worse problems, you are able to:

- find the right coping mechanisms for specific stressors,
- continue being productive despite stress,
- maintain healthy relationships with people around you,
- fulfill your multiple roles without sacrificing the quality of your performance, and
- slowly work towards long-term stress management.

On the other hand, if you keep making mistakes in stress management, you will:

- become a less productive and effective worker,
- get stuck in a cycle of chasing deadlines, causing more stress,
- be unable to show up for other people,
- postpone stress and its symptoms instead of actually solving them, and
- be unable to achieve your goals and delay success.

You want to enforce an effective coping strategy, so you won't suffer from these consequences. The only way to avoid common stress management mistakes is to know what they are so that you can apply the proper solutions.

12.2 Common Stress Management Mistakes

Based on personal experience and conversations with other women, I have observed six common stress management mistakes:

1. You procrastinate.
2. You overwork yourself.
3. You go with the flow.
4. You don't take time to recharge.
5. You isolate yourself from people.
6. You withdraw from your interests.

Let's discuss each of these mistakes, beginning with procrastination. Procrastination takes many shapes. For some people, they postpone doing any work.

Because of stress, they decide to take a break right when they have a lot of tasks to complete. On the other hand, some people do what I call selective procrastination. They still work, but they prioritize less stressful tasks (mostly Level 4 tasks) instead of completing more urgent and important tasks.

Overworking yourself is also a common stress management mistake. Sometimes, there isn't enough time to meet deadlines and/or to balance different roles and responsibilities. As a result, you try to cram as many tasks as possible in a day. The problem with working too much is that you run the risk of being burned out. It isn't a sustainable way to manage stress, and it won't be a productive solution in the long run.

To manage stress, some people just go with the flow. Instead of prioritizing tasks using the technique that I taught you in Chapter 1, you just do whatever is in front of you. The problem with going with the flow is that you'll eventually run out of time to complete urgent and important tasks. You may even realize that you've been working backwards (from lowest to highest priority), so you end up procrastinating.

When your schedule is too busy, you forget to rest and slow down. Everything is in full speed because you've got deadlines to chase. But a car can't keep running if it runs out of gas. It doesn't matter if it's a Lamborghini or a Ferrari—it will stop in the middle of the highway once that fuel tank goes dry. So, don't expect yourself, a human being, to be able to keep working when you're drained of energy.

I've mentioned several times in earlier chapters that isolation is an effect of stress. But it is a common mistake in stress management too. Some people, though they recognize that isolation is not productive in terms of managing stress, still choose to be alone and refuse to seek help. If your tendency is to hide and cancel social plans until you're in a less stressed state, you're doing it wrong.

The last common stress management mistake that I've observed in myself and women I know is that we have a tendency to withdraw from our interests when we're under a lot of pressure. For instance, I put off working out when I feel stressed. Instead, I eat fast food and drink alcohol to try to make myself feel better even though I know that these "coping mechanisms" just make me feel worse about myself. Instead of taking advantage of the physical and mental benefits of exercise, I become more sedentary when I'm stressed. I also binge watch a lot of television shows in an effort to make myself happy. But I'm only putting off the inevitable and, in the process, making my stress level less manageable.

12.3 Foolproof Solutions for Common Stress Management Mistakes

In this section, I want us to take a closer look at every common stress management mistake and discuss actionable steps on how to solve each. These foolproof solutions will ensure that you're not tempted to follow toxic behaviors that aggravate your stress level.

1. You procrastinate.

    - To avoid procrastination, complete tasks based on urgency and importance. Use the prioritization technique that I taught you earlier so that you can better manage your time and, as a result, your stress level.

- Take short breaks throughout the day to avoid feeling uninspired and unmotivated.

2. You overwork yourself.

    - Avoid procrastination so you don't cram all of your urgent and important tasks in a short amount of time.

    - Do one thing that boosts your energy. You can take a warm bath with all of your favorite products or treat yourself to a night out with friends. You should learn to balance your responsibilities with activities that make you happy and rejuvenate your physical and mental state.

    - Stop believing in the idea that you need to overachieve in all of your roles. Unlike what society has taught us, we don't need to please everyone. It's okay to say no. It's okay to not make commitments. You must also prioritize your well-being once in a while.

3. You go with the flow.

    - You might think that going with the flow is an effective coping mechanism, but it only works in the short run. Putting off high-stress tasks is not effective. Eventually, you'll be way more stressed than you are right now. Like the first two mistakes, the solution for this one is to use the prioritization technique that we've talked about.

    - Create a monthly, weekly, and daily overview of your tasks. A monthly overview gives you a general idea of how to manage your time and resources while a weekly and daily overview helps you in creating a more specific plan of action.

4. You don't take time to recharge.

    - Turn your alone time into a habit. Allocate at least two hours a week for self-care.

- Do activities that stimulate your mind and body. Like we discussed in Chapter 5, you need to nurture both of them to remain a productive human being.

- Get enough sleep at night and drink at least two liters of water every day. Rest and hydration are simple steps that you can take to recharge.

5. You isolate yourself from people.

    - Ask for help when you need it. At work, ask your boss if you can have someone to help you with a stressful project. At home, delegate chores to members of the household. There's no good reason to shoulder all of the homecare responsibilities when you're not the only person who lives in the house.

    - Stress tends to make us grumpy, which we can then project onto other people. So, don't just avoid isolating yourself— you should also avoid transferring onto other people, especially if they're your support system.

6. You withdraw from your interests.

    o Make time for your hobbies. Don't stop working out. Don't stop showing up to Wine Night Wednesday with the girls. Don't stop reading books. These activities are good outlets for stress. When you participate in these examples, you are able to improve your physical fitness, maintain your social life, and stimulate your mental capability.

Your Quick-Start Action Step: Identify at least one common stress management mistake that you always do, and choose at least one foolproof solution to address it from the previous section.

Chapter 13: Tools and Apps to Use

Chapter 13: Tools and Apps You Can Use

Remember what I said earlier about how it's been challenging for us to keep up with the growing demands of the modern world? Like everything we know, there's a good side and a bad side to scientific advancements. On the one hand, it may sometimes feel like we're lagging behind technological developments. On the other hand, technology has led to the creation of mobile apps that help us better manage our schedule and activities, which we can then use to alleviate stressors and change toxic habits. I guess you can say that the modern world is self-correcting—it's creating new problems but it also provides us with new tools to solve them.

In this chapter, I want to focus on the good side of technology. I am going to give you a list of the best tools and apps that you can use for stress management.

13.1 Tools and Apps for Stress Management

I am currently using mobile tools and apps for three

main reasons: meditation, productivity, and financial management. I have found that these are three areas where I need help the most, and I believe that they form a great foundation for those who are just starting to incorporate tools and apps into their long-term stress management strategy. Most women I know also struggle with taking care of their mental health, maintaining their productivity level, and managing their finances. In the last section of this chapter, you will find which apps I have found the most useful for these areas.

However, I should note that not all of you who are reading this book will be able to manage your stressors by only using the apps that I have listed in this chapter. Some of you may require other types of apps. There are apps that block distractions so that you can maximize efficiency, that help you in developing better habits, and that keep your notes organized. If you think you need more tools after reading this chapter, I encourage you to do your own research on finding the best apps for the areas where you need help the most.

13.2 Benefits of Stress Management

Tools and Apps

When you use tools and apps for stress management, especially those that target the three areas that I mentioned earlier, you will be able to enjoy the following benefits:

- Meditation apps will help you clear your mind, enhance your focus, and manage your anxiety on a day-to-day basis. They will also encourage you to incorporate meditation in your daily habits so that you can gain long-term mental health benefits.

- Productivity apps will help you in better managing your time and tasks so that you can always be on schedule.

- Financial management apps will help those like me who have always struggled with staying on budget.

13.3 Best Tools and Apps for Stress Management

I'm dividing this section into the three key areas that

we identified earlier. I have listed three of the best apps for each category. I have also given each app an overall rating out of 10 based on their features, pros and cons, and price so that you can make an informed decision. Let's start with meditation apps.

Meditation Apps

Meditation apps are my favorite stress management tool because they help me alleviate stress and its symptoms in real time. My top three meditation apps are Sanvello, GPS for the Soul, and Headspace.

1. Sanvello

Sanvello is a comprehensive app providing science-based solutions that are designed to make you feel happier and less anxious over time. You can also set other mental health goals while you set up the app. The premium version costs $8.99 per month. Its features include:

- meditation guides,
- health habit tracker,
- mood tracker,

- built-in journal,
- support communities, and
- guided journeys.

Pros:

- Sanvello has a user-friendly interface that's easy to understand. Even with a lot of features, the format is clean and the controls are intuitive.

- The free version already comes with a lot of cool features, so you don't need to purchase the premium version.

- The community tab has a chat feature that allows you to reach out to other people who are dealing with the same problems.

Cons:

- I have been using Sanvello for several weeks now and, to be honest, I haven't seen a single downside to this app. I like its features, and I think the app offers a comprehensive solution to stress and other mental health problems.

I give Sanvello an overall rating of 10 out of 10.

2. The Mindfulness App

The Mindfulness App is a great app for meditation. Not only does it have guided meditation courses, it also helps you turn meditation into a habit. The premium version costs $9.99 per month or $54.99 for a year. Its features include:

- five-day introduction to mindfulness,
- meditations taught by professionals, and
- guided and silent timed sessions.

Pros:

- When you unlock premium, you'll get access to 250+ additional guided meditations.
- There are meditations that last for three minutes to half an hour, so you can choose a session that works best for your schedule.
- Sessions can be downloaded so you can use them offline.

Cons:

- The Mindfulness App does what it says on the tin—it's an app for mindfulness. If you're looking for other features (like Sanvello's built-in journal and support communities), you might be disappointed.

I give The Mindfulness App an overall rating of seven out of 10.

3. Headspace

Headspace is my favorite meditation app. I've been using it for years now. It has guided meditations that target different problem areas and a Sleep tab that focuses on helping you in getting better sleep at night. The premium version costs $12.99 a month or $95.88 for a whole year. Its features include:

- Everybody Headspace (livestream practice for premium users),
- Sleepcasts, Sleep Sounds, and Wind Downs,
- meditation for kids, and
- meditation tracker.

Pros:

- The Headspace Library is constantly updated, but it currently contains hundreds of meditation courses for managing stress and anxiety, falling asleep and waking up, and overcoming life challenges. It also has meditation courses focused on performance mindset, personal growth, work and productivity, kids and parenting, sports, physical health, and students.

- Like The Mindfulness App, the durations of meditation courses have a wide range, so you can choose which exercise best fits your schedule.

- The Kids Calm courses are for all ages, but they particularly teach young kids about the importance of meditation. This feature is especially useful for moms who want to help their children learn how to manage stress and anxiety at an early age.

Cons:

- Headspace is the most expensive meditation app on this list.

- The free version is somewhat limited. If you want to get access to specialized meditation courses, you need to purchase the premium version.

I give Headspace an overall rating of eight out of 10.

Productivity Apps

Productivity apps help me to stay focused on my tasks and to streamline my schedule so that I can be as efficient as possible. My top three productivity apps are Evernote, Actions by Moleskine, and Todoist.

1. Evernote

Evernote is a cloud-based tool that allows you to keep your notes organized and secure. I love using this app because I usually have bursts of inspiration about things that I want to write about when I'm commuting or running errands. With Evernote, I have all of my ideas in one place.

Evernote offers three plans: Basic, Premium, and Business. The Basic plan is free, the Premium plan costs $7.99 per month, and the Business plan costs $14.99 per user per month. Its features include:

- to-do list,

- scan documents,

- insert photos,

- sketch drawings, diagrams, and graphs,

- templates,

- offline access (for Premium and Business),

- team collaboration and presentation mode (for Business), and

- 60mb, 1gb, and 10gb monthly upload limit.

Pros:

- For personal use, the Basic plan is more than enough. I personally use this plan because it has all the features that I need to keep my ideas organized.

- Evernote has a simple and intuitive interface that you'll find easy to use.

- You can also use Evernote to create schedules, meal plans, and itineraries.

Cons:

- If you're planning to use Evernote for business, you need to pay $14.99 per month for at least two people.

- Evernote has free alternatives like Microsoft OneNote and Google Keep that have higher storage limits.

I give Evernote an overall rating of seven out of 10.

2. Actions by Moleskine

Actions by Moleskine is the simplest mobile app planner that I have ever used. I love it because of how easy it is to use. If you're familiar with bullet journals, it follows the same ideology, which is not a surprise since Moleskine is probably the most popular brand used by dedicated bullet journal fans. The premium version costs $1.99 per month or $11.99 for a whole year. Its features include:

- Action Cards (with schedule option),

- Lists to organize Action Cards (with color coding),

- repeating actions,
- iOS share extension,
- Siri integration, and
- swipe to delete, complete, or set reminders for Action Cards.

Pros:

- You can create unlimited Action Cards with the premium version.
- All Action Cards are synced automatically to the cloud.
- This app breaks down your week in a detailed but not complicated way.
- You can definitely use Actions by Moleskine within the context of the prioritization technique that I taught you in Chapter 1. Use the color-coding feature to distinguish each priority level.

Cons:

- Although available in the Google Play Store, Actions by Moleskine works best with iOS phones.

I give Actions by Moleskine an overall rating of eight out of 10.

3. Todoist

Todoist is a more comprehensive productivity app with a wider range of features than Actions. Like Evernote, it offers three plans: Basic, Premium, and Business. The Basic plan is free, the Premium plan costs $3 per month billed annually, and the Business plan costs $5 per user per month billed annually (or $6 per user per month billed monthly). Its features include: Its features include:

- color-coded priority levels,
- recurring schedule,
- project section and sub-tasks,
- task delegation (for Business), and
- productivity tracker (for Premium and Business).

Pros:

- What I love most about Todoist is that it helps users build habits, thanks to its productivity tracker feature. You'll be able to see your streaks and measure your progress using this app.

- Todoist also has a task delegation feature. If your family members all download the app, you can assign chores and other tasks with a few taps.

- This mobile app also has a desktop version so you can use it on your laptop.

Cons:

- You need to purchase the Premium version if you want to enjoy most of the features that I love about this app.

I give Todoist an overall rating of seven out of 10.

Financial Management Apps

The financial management apps that I included in this list allow you to create a budget and help you to stick to it. My top three financial management apps are Mint, You Need a Budget, and Mvelopes.

1. Mint

Mint brings together all of your accounts, so you have an overview of your financial status. You can also integrate all of your bills as well as your investments within the app.

Its features include:

- monthly bill tracker and reminder,
- budget plan,
- net worth tracker,
- expense categories,
- financial goals,
- reports and trends,
- free credit score, and
- investments.

Pros:

- Mint is absolutely free!

- The financial goals feature gives you something to work on. You can set a monthly spending limit, set aside an emergency fund, and reach a savings goal.

- The free credit score feature shows you how strong your credit score is and what you can do to improve it.

Cons:

- Mint is only available in the United States and Canada.

- You can only plan budgets for the current month.

- Mint may be too detailed for some. It has a lot of moving aspects, and it may not be as intuitive as the other apps on this list if your main concern is budgeting.

I give Mint an overall rating of six out of 10.

2. You Need a Budget (YNAB)

You Need a Budget is a popular budgeting tool that forces you to account for every dollar that you earn and that helps you in forming long-term financial goals. Its features include:

- bank syncing,
- real-time updates,
- goal tracking,
- financial reports, and
- 100+ free, live, online workshops.

Pros:

- The interface is highly intuitive. It's not confusing or overwhelming like Mint can be.
- I love the whole idea behind You Need a Budget. Giving each dollar a "job" means you can account for each dollar you spend or save. You can clearly see where you overspend so that you can identify ways to improve how you manage your finances.

- The free workshops have also helped me a lot in improving my personal financial management skills. You can learn about how to save for retirement, how to do your taxes, and how to avoid making budgeting mistakes.

Cons:

- You Need a Budget is available for a 34-day free trial period, but you'll have to purchase it for $84 per year afterwards.

- You Need a Budget doesn't track investments.

I give You Need a Budget an overall rating of eight out of 10.

3. Mvelopes

Mvelopes follows the envelope budgeting technique, i.e., you categorize your expenses, allocate a budget for each category, and are only allowed to spend that budget for the whole month.

Mvelopes offers two plans: Basic and Plus. The Basic plan costs $5.99 per month or $59.99 per year, while the Plus plan costs $18.99 per month or $189.99 per year. Its features include:

- income cash pool overview,
- credit card payments,
- account transfers,
- customizable envelopes,
- spending plan,
- transactions tracker, and
- bills tracker.

Pros:

- Mvelopes gives you a detailed overview of all of your expenses. It lets you assign a budget for each expense and will let you know if you've overspent on a category.
- Mvelopes tracks your credit card purchases and includes it in your spending report so you don't run out of funds in your checking account.
- You can use the envelope budgeting technique without having to withdraw cash.

Cons:

- Mvelopes is available for a 30-day free trial period, but you'll have to purchase one of the plans afterwards.

- Like You Need a Budget, Mvelopes doesn't track investments.

- Mvelopes is not available worldwide.

I give Mvelopes an overall rating of six out of 10.

Your Quick-Start Action Step: Download at least one app for each area from the list in the previous section. Use these apps daily for at least three weeks. I'm a firm believer of the idea that you can form a habit if you continuously do it for 21 days straight. For each week that passes, take down a few notes of how each app has helped you. What features are most beneficial? How are they not serving you? At the end of the trial, you can decide whether the app stays on your phone or not.

Chapter 14: More Time Management Strategies

Chapter 14: More Time Management Strategies

We only have 24 hours a day and we spend a third of it sleeping. If you're like me, you also have a nine-to-five office job, which accounts for another third. For the last third of the day, we try to fit in as many responsibilities as we can. We have kids to raise, a house to maintain, and relationships to nurture. How are we supposed to fit all of these things in just one day? Do we even have time left to take care of ourselves?

Time management has always been challenging for me, and it often causes my stress level to rapidly rise to an unmanageable magnitude. I panic about all the things I need to do and how little time I have left to do them. Sometimes, I reach a point where I can't do any work because I'm completely burned out.

When this happens, I am unable to write. I can't perform well at work. I don't even want to spend time with my family. I stay in bed, curled up like a baby in her mother's belly, while I suffer from a pounding migraine that feels like it will split my skull in two. To be honest, I still feel like this once in a while. Even with all the stress management techniques that I have learned throughout the years, I am yet to master time management as a skill.

But I want to work on it and I want to work on it with all of you. So, let's talk about the importance of time management as well as a few strategies that we can employ to improve this skill. This chapter means so much to me because I still struggle with balancing my roles apropos of the amount of time I have.

A friend of mine, the same one who encouraged me to write this book, said that she also finds it difficult to efficiently manage her time simply due to the fact that she has so many responsibilities to juggle.

I think we share this common struggle as women, so I believe this chapter will help a lot of you who are reading this book.

14.1 Time Management

Time management is a process of distributing your time among different activities. To be effective in all of your roles, you need to learn how to manage your time more efficiently. But I know that this is easier said than done. As I mentioned earlier, I still haven't completely cracked the code when it comes to time management.

And it's not always because I'm burned out. There are days when it feels like there just isn't enough time. The list of things to do is just too long for one single day. Even if I work for the whole day without taking a break, it seems impossible to fit all of my tasks within the time that I don't spend sleeping at night.

The problem is we can't be successful if we don't master time management. It's a significant skill that we use in our daily lives. Without it, we will always feel like we're running at full speed to get things done.

14.2 Importance of Time Management

Why is time management so important? Well, if we learn to distribute our time more efficiently, we will be able to:

- increase productivity,
- meet deadlines on time,
- improve work performance,

- spend more time with friends and family,
- have time for self-care,
- achieve life and career goals, and
- decrease stress levels.

If we don't learn how to effectively manage our time, we will:

- feel drained and burned out,
- have no time for hobbies and relationships,
- suffer from chronic stress,
- experience lower life satisfaction,
- be unable to achieve life and career goals, and
- miss opportunities for personal and career growth.

14.3 Time Management Strategies

I want to make time management simple for everyone, including me, so I have devised a five-step action plan:

1. Manage your time on a weekly basis.

2. Create a morning routine.

3. Limit recreational activities during the weekdays.

4. Avoid bringing work home during the weekends.

5. Work on at least one Level 1 task for the day before 10 a.m.

Let's discuss each step in more detail.

1. Manage your time on a weekly basis.

Why should you manage your time on a weekly basis? Well, managing your time per every 24 hours (daily) is too restrictive, but doing it per every 720 hours (monthly) is too confusing. So, zoom in on your week: there are 168 hours in seven days. If we subtract eight hours of sleep a night, we still have 112 hours left. If you work 40 hours a week, you still have 72 hours left for other activities. Doesn't that look like a lot of time to divide among your different tasks?

If your job permits it, you can work longer hours on

select days and then go home earlier on an equal number of days. For example, you can work for 10 hours every Monday and Tuesday and leave two hours early on Thursday and Friday. You still meet the 40-hour work week requirement, but you have more time on Thursday and Friday to do other activities like bonding with your family.

Don't forget to allocate at least two hours each week to self-care and similar activities. If you're in a relationship, you should also make time for at least one date night every week to maintain intimacy.

2. Create a morning routine.

I am not a morning person. I don't like waking up early. If I can wake up at noon every day, I will. But research has shown that early birds do get the worm. They are happier and more productive on average than night owls.

When I first read about this research, I shook my head in disagreement. But then I thought about it again, and I realized that I do get more things done when I wake up early. This is because I usually get tired late in the afternoon, so I become less productive when I work through the night. It's just biology—it's my body's way of preparing itself for sleep.

So, create a morning routine that helps you wake up earlier. I've actually been trying to wake up early for the past few months. I've been getting up at 6 a.m. on weekdays and at 7:00 a.m. on weekends. Let me share with you the routine I have created for myself.

- I have found that washing my face with cold water and my favorite skin product makes me feel more awake.

- I make coffee using a coffee dripper instead of a machine. If you're familiar with the former, you need to boil water to pour over the coffee grounds. So, I set the kettle on the stove and, while waiting for it to whistle, I sit down by the window and perform a quick meditation exercise. It only takes five minutes to start the day with a clear and peaceful mind.

- When the water boils, I make my coffee and cook breakfast for everyone. I actually enjoy cooking, so this is a great start for me.

- I eat breakfast with my family every day.

- I take showers in the evening, so I don't need to rush in the morning to dry and style my hair. Before leaving the house, I just need to brush my teeth, do my makeup, and get dressed. I also plan my outfits the night before, so I don't need to think about it in the morning.

- Before I leave the house, I write three things that I want to accomplish during the day. They shouldn't be related to work or domestic responsibilities. For example, I might want to squeeze in a quick run after work, call my mom, and have a drink and catch up with a friend before going home.

3. Limit recreational activities during the weekdays.

I waste a lot of time watching television and scrolling through my phone each day. It's unbelievable how much time I spend doing these senseless things that offer short-term happiness. If you're always tempted to waste your time like me, I want you to ask yourself these questions: "Does this activity benefit me in the long run? Will it take me closer to my life and career goals?" If you answer no to both of these questions, then why should you still do it?

4. Avoid bringing work home during the weekends.

I've been trying to avoid working at home because I already spend 40 hours a week at the office. I deserve to have a full life and you do too. So, manage your time like you're planning your budget. You've already allocated a specific amount to work—if you use more hours for it, you're going to eat into your budget for other activities. Is it a good trade-off?

5. Work on at least one Level 1 task for the day before 10 a.m.

Working on an urgent and important task at the start of the day sets the tone for the rest of it. When you feel accomplished in the morning, you create a ripple effect that motivates you to complete other tasks. As a result, you become more driven and productive.

Your Quick-Start Action Step: Create a morning routine that works for you and stick to it for 21 days. Like I mentioned in the previous chapter, you can form a habit if you repeat doing it for at least three weeks straight.

Chapter 15: Simplifying Your Life

Chapter 15: Simplifying Your Life

I've mentioned repeatedly in the past that stress usually stems from our hectic schedules and fast-paced lives. We're always rushing to get things done, so we can achieve long-term goals as soon as we can. We barely take a moment to slow down and be grateful for what we already have because we're always running towards the next thing.

But what if we simplify our lives? What if we stop overworking ourselves? What if we choose to live in the moment and to appreciate the little things? Would our lives be less stressful? I think you already know the answer.

15.1 Living a Simpler Life

Living a simpler life means getting rid of possessions and behaviors that don't contribute to your overall wellness. It means being happy about living with less instead of always trying to accumulate things. It means experiencing life as it unfolds instead of constantly taking photos that you can post on social media.

A simpler life doesn't have to mean that you deprive yourself of things that make you happy. But I want you to stop measuring your self-worth on material possessions. If you embrace a simpler lifestyle, you'll realize that most of your stressors root from materialism. You work too hard because you want to buy things to fill your house with. You've subscribed to the idea that nothing is ever enough—that there's always room for more. I can't really blame you if you do think like this. Society has conditioned us to worship consumerism, and so we're inclined to always want more than what we need.

Remember this: There's a difference between being driven and being greedy. Look around you. Do all the things you own bring you long-term happiness? What percentage of your possessions were bought on a whim? How many things did you buy for status? Is your house cluttered with things that you don't need or use?

Physical and mental exhaustion, stress, and long hours of work that you could have spent doing more valuable things, like spending time with your family, are the price of materialism. Is it worth it?

15.2 Beauty in Simplicity

Believe it or not, there is beauty in simplicity. Even though you have to let go of some of your material possessions, you gain more important things in the process. By adopting a more minimalist lifestyle, you will be able to:

- work towards financial freedom,
- spend more quality time with friends and family,
- declutter and organize your living space,
- enjoy moments rather than documenting them on your phone,
- balance career and life goals with overall wellness,
- seek a greater purpose,
- prioritize what's important in life, and
- feel happier, more grateful, and more content.

I know that it's hard to unlearn what society has

taught us. Making the change towards minimalism is a long process. But trust me—it's a journey worth taking.

15.3 How to Simplify Your Life

Before I share some actionable steps that will help you live more minimalistically, I want to set one ground rule first: you don't actually have to adopt minimalism as a lifestyle.

Yes, that's right. I don't want you to sell your car or remove decor items from your home. I don't want you to purge your closet and just keep a capsule wardrobe. Like I said earlier, I don't want you to deprive yourself of things that make you happy.

I just want you to use minimalism as a guiding principle. I want you to make decisions with intention. If something doesn't serve your long-term goals or overall wellness, learn to say no.

Here are a few ways to simplify your life:

1. Declutter your space. Remove all things that you haven't used in the past year. You can also use the KonMari method—ask yourself: "Does

this spark joy?" If an item doesn't immediately bring you happiness and you haven't used it in a while, you most likely won't be using it in the near future. So, there's really no point in keeping it. Donate or sell items that are still in good shape, so they can find new homes where they can be utilized.

2. Keep your space organized. A messy environment is not conducive for rest or productivity. Take a day or two to find a dedicated space for everything you own so that you can just return all items to their home every time you use them.

3. In every purchasing decision, ask yourself: "Do I need this?" For example, do you really need to buy the new iPhone if your current phone is still working? How many months will you have to pay for credit for this new gadget? Isn't it wiser to put that money towards something with more meaning? Maybe you can put it in your savings fund or towards a trip that you've been dreaming to take. Money is one of the biggest stressors for a lot of people. By being

more intentional with your purchases, you can work towards financial security.

4. Step away from social media once in a while. I recommend that you completely unplug from technology once every two weeks, which just amounts to two internet-free days every month. I have found that scrolling through social media is a mindless way to waste time. More importantly, studies have shown that social media is not good for our mental health. In fact, social media obsession and anxiety are considered a mental health problem now.

5. My last tip for simplifying life is to let go of toxic thoughts and feelings that weigh you down. Life gets more complicated when we keep carrying resentment, anger, and contempt in our hearts. So, try to make amends with at least one person who has hurt you or whom you've hurt. Find a way to settle your differences and seek forgiveness for each other.

Your Quick-Start Action Step: Donate or throw away at least 10 things that you haven't used in the past year. This exercise will get the ball rolling on decluttering your space and letting go of possessions that don't serve you anymore.

BONUS Chapter: Stress Management for Working Moms

Bonus Chapter: Stress Management for Working Moms

Stress management takes a whole other level if you're a working mom. I know how difficult it is to balance my career and my family. As much as I want to be present at home, I need to work. And when I need to spend some time alone, I feel overwhelmed with mommy guilt.

But I think I have found a healthy balance between these two roles. In this bonus chapter, I want to help other working moms with a simple stress management guide that's tailored for us.

16.1 The Working Mom Life

According to the data, 70% of moms with children below 18 years old are in the labor force, with 40% of American families relying on the mother as the primary breadwinner. We spend an average of 25 hours on paid work and 14 hours on childcare per week. In addition, women are also 21% more likely to feel pressured to be an involved parent than men.

I've heard a lot of stories from fellow working moms

who have felt this pressure. Because of traditional gender expectations, we are facing pressures both at home and at work. It feels like we're always making a choice between these two roles. Do we work hard to provide for our families and sacrifice our time with them? Or do we spend more time with them and sacrifice opportunities for career development?

Mommy guilt is another powerful stressor. As working moms, we feel guilty about leaving our children at home, spending less time with them, and missing out on watching them grow. Forget about spending alone time—we're wired to think that our rest days should be spent bonding with our children and partner rather than finding time to ourselves.

16.2 Balancing Family, Career, and Identity

Imagine standing on a platform and holding a tray with three glasses of water—all three of them are full to the brim. When you're stressed, it feels like the platform you're standing on is shaking and shrinking. The more you feel stressed, the shakier and smaller the platform gets. The shakier and smaller the platform gets, the harder it is to keep the glasses full.

These three glasses represent our family life, our career, and our sense of self. When stress shakes up our lives and makes our world feel smaller, it's harder to feel fulfilled in all three of these aspects. Eventually, we'll fall off the platform, spilling all three.

Like every other woman, working moms need an effective stress coping mechanism in order to live a healthier and fuller life. I think working moms need stress management more than anyone does because stress doesn't just affect us—it affects our families and jobs too. We're not just spilling one glass—we're spilling all three.

16.3 Stress Management Guide for Working Moms

Stress management is an important topic, and I have four pieces of advice for my fellow working moms:

1. Remember who you are. Your identity as a woman must not revolve around your role as a mom and your career. You need to have three

glasses, i.e., your identity must be independent from these two roles. Otherwise, you won't have a place to seek refuge when home and work stressors become too much.

2. Practice goal setting. I taught you about SMART goal setting in Chapter 3. To quickly recap, SMART means setting specific, manageable, attainable, relevant, and time-based goals for each aspect of your life.

3. Surround yourself with a reliable support system. The first person you should look to for support is your partner. If both of you are working, you should share domestic responsibilities equally. When you feel stressed about work, you should be able to share your problems with each other. However, you should be careful not to catch each other's stress. My husband and I have found two phrases that clearly convey what we need: "I need attention" and "I need space." When one of us says the former, we give them undivided attention for an hour. When one of us says the latter, the other manages the kids and the

house for an hour to give one of us an opportunity to have alone time. Aside from your partner, you should also find support from other people outside your marriage. I have found that spending time with other moms (preferably with a bottle of red wine and a cheese platter), reduces my stress level significantly. We get to vent about our work and life problems to each other. As a result, we avoid transferring our stress to our kids and partners.

4. Be kind to yourself. This is the most important advice that I can give to you. Even if we don't mean to, we can be our biggest critics. Mommy guilt is proof of our tendency to self-flagellate. To prevent stress from building up, you should try to be more compassionate towards yourself and what you believe to be your incompetencies. No mother is perfect because we're all human. The best we can do is to try our best for ourselves, our families, and our careers.

Your Quick-Start Action Step: Using the SMART

technique, list a set of goals for yourself, your family life, and your career. Then identify actionable steps that you can take in order to achieve these goals.

Conclusion

Being a woman in this day and age involves facing a lot of pressure to overachieve in all aspects of our lives. We are juggling multiple roles while also dealing with traditional gender expectations, which can cause an enormous amount of stress that leads to more serious mental health problems.

At the beginning of this book, I set out to provide stress management solutions to help readers cope with both acute and chronic stress. The strategies that I have presented can be applied to different situations by different types of women.

In Chapter 1, we defined stress and the four factors that cause women to experience more physical and mental symptoms than men. Gender roles, gender traits, cognitive appraisal, and biological factors explain why stress manifests differently between the two sexes. We also talked about the common symptoms of stress in women and why you need an effective stress management strategy. At the end of the chapter, I taught you three general techniques that you can apply in all areas of life: the SMART technique, the prioritization technique, and the Serenity Prayer.

In Chapter 2, we talked about chronic stress, its symptoms, and the physical and mental health problems that can stem from it. We also discussed the common sources of long-term stress which include traumatic events, financial problems, and relationship problems. Then I gave you actionable steps on how to deal with chronic stress. The four-step process includes assessing whether your stress is chronic or not, determining where it comes from, talking about it with someone, and finding a way to deal with it given its respective source. Before I closed the chapter, I gave you some stress management tips in relation to the four common sources of chronic stress.

Chapter 3 focused on purpose and how it ties to your overall wellness. You learned about the importance of having a clear purpose and why you need a wellness plan. Then I taught you a five-step wellness plan strategy which involves using the SMART method to create goals and identify actionable steps for different areas in your life. Aside from goal setting, your wellness plan also involves preparing a contingency plan for unforeseen events.

We talked about how stress can cause emotional distress (like irritability and anger) and psychological disorders (like anxiety and depression) in the next chapter. I established the importance of recognizing when stress is causing negative emotions. Then we discussed how regret, old ideas, righteousness, and blaming thoughts for behaviors can lead to a negative mindset. To help you overcome these challenges and change your mindset for the better, I taught you how to understand your emotions, find an outlet, show yourself kindness, express yourself in a more compassionate manner when in disagreement with someone, face unhealthy thoughts head on, and change patterns of behavior that lead to negative emotions.

In Chapter 5, we looked into mind and body wellness and the importance of a holistic approach to well-being. You learned that you need both your physical and mental state to be in good shape for you to remain productive and improve your quality of life. I also gave you practical tips on how to take care of your mental wellness, which include mindful breathing, meditation, journaling, self-care, and hobbies, as well as your physical wellness which include yoga, exercise, stretching, getting a full night's sleep, and drinking enough water.

The next two chapters focused on dealing and relieving stress in the workplace and at home. We identified work stressors (i.e., work content and work context) and home stressors (i.e., work spillover and multiple roles). We also talked about how stress in these areas affects you and the people around you and how you can manage them effectively.

In Chapter 9, I gave you quick stress management techniques that you can perform in one to three minutes. These exercises will help alleviate stress when you need to focus on important tasks at work and home.

Chapters 10 and 11 focused on rejuvenation through spending alone time and taking vacations. These practices will help relieve chronic stress and give you opportunities to recharge so that you can be the best version of yourself. I gave you a few ideas on what you can do during your alone time as well as some tips on how to plan trips stress free.

The succeeding chapter deals with common stress management mistakes that people make. Procrastinating, overworking, going with the flow, not taking time to recharge, isolating yourself, and withdrawing from interests are surefire ways to make your stress even worse. At the end of the chapter, I gave you foolproof solutions on how to avoid each of these mistakes.

In Chapter 13, I gave you a list of tools and apps that you can use to manage stress. I included three apps each for meditation, productivity, and financial management because I have found that most women need help in these areas. I have personally tested these apps myself and gave them an overall rating based on their features, pros and cons, and price. For meditation, my favorites are Sanvello, The Mindfulness App, and Headspace. For productivity, my favorites are Evernote, Actions by Moleskine, and Todoist. Lastly, my favorites for financial management are Mint, You Need a Budget, and Mvelopes.

In Chapter 14, I shared with you my biggest struggle when it comes to stress management—time management. I know that most of you, no matter if you're a mom, a career woman, or a student, struggle with it too. To help all of us more effectively manage our time, I came up with a five-step action plan. I believe that managing time on a weekly basis and creating a morning routine are great solutions, but finding a good balance between personal life and work will make us a lot better in terms of time management. Working on a Level 1 task at the start of your day will also make you feel more productive for the rest of the day, so you are not rushing to get things done for the rest of it.

We touched on the subject of minimalism in the last chapter of the book. I hope I was able to show you how a simpler life can help eliminate stressors and make you feel more happy and content. To help you get started, I gave you five ways to simplify your life. Decluttering your space, keeping it organized, being intentional in your purchasing decisions, unplugging from technology, and letting go of toxic thoughts and feelings will lead to a significant positive change in how you live.

Before ending our conversation, I wanted to dedicate

a bonus chapter for working moms. Hopefully, the stress management guide that I included in this bonus chapter will help you balance your family life, career, and identity. Don't forget who you are and to celebrate your independence. Practice goal setting to organize all three aspects of your life. Surround yourself with a reliable support system because no one on this planet can walk through life alone. Lastly, show yourself kindness and forgive yourself when you make mistakes.

If there's one thing that I want you to take away from this book, just read the previous sentence again. I want you to read it over and over again until it becomes true. The world is cruel enough on its own. It's your responsibility to love yourself and to accept who you are, flaws and all. Even Superman has a weakness, so why can't you, Superwoman, have one too? When you learn to be kind to yourself, you'll learn to manage stress more effectively as a result.

References:

American Psychological Association. (n.d.) Dealing with financial stress. Retrieved from https://www.apa.org/helpcenter/holiday-stress-finances

American Psychological Association. (n.d.). Gender and stress. Retrieved from https://www.apa.org/news/press/releases/stress/2010/gender-stress

American Psychological Association (n.d.). Stress: The different kinds of stress. Retrieved from https://www.apa.org/helpcenter/stress-kinds

Association for Psychological Science. (n.d.) Negative emotions in response to daily stress take a toll on long-term mental health. Retrieved from https://www.psychologicalscience.org/news/releases/negative-emotions-in-response-to-daily-stress-take-a-toll-on-long-term-mental-health.html

Bernstein, R. (2016). The mind and mental health: How stress affects the brain. Retrieved from https://www.tuw.edu/health/how-stress-affects-the-brain/

Cripps, K. (2018). World's 10 most popular tourist destinations (and their future rivals). Retrieved from https://edition.cnn.com/travel/article/world-most-popular-destinations-2017/index.html

Daskal, L. (2016). 4 scientific reasons vacations are good for your health. Retrieved from https://www.inc.com/lolly-daskal/4-scientific-reasons-why-vacation-is-awesome-for-you.html

Duberman, A. (2014). Women feel more stress at home than at work, study finds. Retrieved from https://www.huffpost.com/

Fader, S. (2018). Social media obsession and anxiety. Retrieved from https://adaa.org/social-media-obsession

Gallup. (2019). *Gallup global emotions.* Washington, DC: Clifton, J.

Geiger, A., Livingston, G., Bialik, K. (2019). 6 facts about U.S. moms. Retrieved from https://www.pewresearch.org/fact-tank/2019/05/08/facts-about-u-s-mothers/#targetText=In%2046%25%20of%20households%20with,24%25)%20are%20solo%20moms.

Gregoire, C. (2014, December 22). 10 ways stress affects women's health. Retrieved from https://www.huffpost.com/

Harvard Medical School. (2018). Understanding stress response. Retrieved from https://www.health.harvard.edu/staying-healthy/understanding-the-stress-response

Heitler, S. (2013). Stress in relationships: 10 sources and their antidotes [Blog post]. Retrieved from https://www.psychologytoday.com/intl/blog/resolution-not-conflict/201305/stress-in-relationships-10-sources-and-their-antidotes

Hoff, A. (2019). Research shows early birds to be happier, more productive than night owls. Retrieved from https://philadelphia.cbslocal.com/2019/02/16/research-shows-early-birds-to-be-happier-more-productive-than-night-owls/

Huang, G. (2018). Men and women aren't promoted by the same people—Here's the difference. *Forbes*. Retrieved from https://www.forbes.com/

Jacobs, M. (n.d.). Stress and a woman's body [Infographic]. Retrieved from https://www.empowher.com/stress/content/infographic-stress-and-womans-body?utm_content=buffer7f224&utm_medium=social&utm_source=twitter.com&utm_campaign=buffer

Johnston, G. (2012). *The effect of meaning and purpose in life on wellness and life satisfaction* (Unpublished doctoral dissertation). Texas Tech University, Lubbock, TX.

Kandola, A. (2018). What are the health effects of chronic stress? Retrieved from https://www.medicalnewstoday.com/articles/323324.php

Kaplin, A. & Anzaldi, L. (2015). New movement in neuroscience: A purpose-driven life.

Cerebrum: The Dana Forum on Brain Science. Retrieved from https://www.dana.org/article/new-movement-in-neuroscience-a-purpose-driven-life/

Lipman, V. (2019, January 9). Workplace trend: Stress is on the rise. *Forbes*. Retrieved from https://www.forbes.com/

Mayor, E. (2015). Gender roles and traits in stress and health. *Frontiers in Psychology, 6*, 779. doi:10.3389/fpsyg.2015.00779

McLeod, S. (2017). Type A and B personality. Retrieved from https://www.simplypsychology.org/personality-a.html

Mind. (2018). Post-traumatic stress disorder. Retrieved from https://www.mind.org.uk/information-support/types-of-mental-health-problems/post-traumatic-stress-disorder-ptsd/causes-of-ptsd/#.XYZKAZMzbjD

Morin, A. (2017). 7 science-backed reasons you should spend more time alone. *Forbes*. Retrieved from https://www.forbes.com/sites/amymorin/2017/08/05/7-science-backed-reasons-you-should-spend-more-time-alone/#53cdb38a1b7e

National Institute of Mental Health. (2016). *5 things you should know about stress* (NIH Publication No. OM 16-4310). Bethesda, MD: Office of Science Policy, Planning and Communications Science Writing, Press, and Dissemination Branch.

Neate, R. (2018). Global pay gap will take 202 years to close, says world economic forum. *The Guardian*. Retrieved from https://www.theguardian.com/

Newman, K. (2016). Could stress be causing your relationship problems? Retrieved from https://greatergood.berkeley.edu/article/item/could_stress_be_causing_your_relationship_problems

Newman, K. (2017). What to do when you feel stuck in negative emotions. Retrieved from https://www.mindful.org/feel-stuck-negative-emotions/

Office on Women's Health. (n.d.). Stress and your health. Retrieved from https://www.womenshealth.gov/mental-health/good-mental-health/stress-and-your-health

Rizzo, C. (2018). Why more travelers are purchasing travel insurance this year. *Travel and Leisure*. Retrieved from https://www.travelandleisure.com/

Robbins, T. (n.d.). How to handle your partner's stress. Retrieved from https://www.tonyrobbins.com/love-relationships/how-to-help-partner-in-times-of-stress/

Santiago, C., Wadsworth, M., & Stump, J. (2011). Socioeconomic status, neighborhood disadvantage, and poverty-related stress: Prospective effects on psychological syndromes among diverse low-income families. *Journal of Economic Psychology 32*(2), 218-230. doi:10.1016/j.joep.2009.10.008

Shrout, R. (2018). What are the effects of stress on a relationship? *Nevada Today.* Retrieved from https://www.unr.edu/nevada-today

Statista Research Department. (2018). Global travel and tourism industry - Statistics & facts. Retrieved from https://www.statista.com/topics/962/global-tourism/

Tartakovsky, M. (2018). 5 benefits of group therapy. Retrieved from https://psychcentral.com/lib/5-benefits-of-group-therapy/

The American Institute of Stress. (n.d.). Workplace stress. Retrieved from https://www.stress.org/workplace-stress

United Nations Statistics Division. (2015). Poverty [PDF]. Retrieved from https://unstats.un.org/unsd/gender/downloads/Ch8_Poverty_info.pdf

Verman, R., Balhara, Y., & Gupta, C. (2011). Gender Differences in Stress Response: Role of Developmental and Biological Determinants. *Industrial Psychiatry Journal, 20*(1), 4-10. doi:10.4103/0972-6748.98407

World Bank. (2018). International tourism, number of arrivals. Retrieved from https://data.worldbank.org/indicator/ST.INT.ARVL?end=2017&start=2007&view=chart

World Health Organization. (2010). *WHO healthy workplace: framework and model: Background and supporting literature and practices*. Geneève, Geneva: Burton, J.

World Health Organization. (n.d.). Stress at the workplace. Retrieved from https://www.who.int/occupational_health/topics/stressatwp/en/

World Vision. (2018). Global poverty: Facts, faqs, and how to help. Retrieved from https://www.worldvision.org/sponsorship-news-stories/global-poverty-facts

www.ingramcontent.com/pod-product-compliance
Lightning Source LLC
Chambersburg PA
CBHW071237070526
44583CB00017B/2222